To Monica!

I is for Ivanova —
The right hand of Vengeance
AKA God
She is Always right —
Listen to her!

Snack Hacks

OVER 100 FAST AND DELICIOUS RECIPES
FOR GAMERS, CODERS,
FREAKS AND GEEKS

CLAUDIA CHRISTIAN
& MARK MICHEL

FLOATING
WORLD PRESS

Copyright © 2019 Claudia Christian & Mark Michel

All rights reserved. No part of this book may be used or reproduced in any manner whatsoever without written permission except in the case of brief quotations embodied in a critical article or review.

Disclaimer: Prepare and cook all recipes in this book with a good dose of common sense. Use correct, functional cooking implements and follow instructions carefully. If you have dietary restrictions or allergies please consult with your doctor before consuming foods prepared in this book.

Floating World Press
www.floatingworldpress.com

10 9 8 7 6 5 4 3 2 1

ISBN: 978-0-6482831-9-5

Cover and interior design by Morgan Buchanan
Cover photography by Nick Mendoza
Edited by Catherine Buchanan

This publication has not been prepared, approved, endorsed or licensced by the author, producer, or owner of any motion picture, television program, book, game, blog or other works referred to herein. This is not an official or licensed publication. Any trademarks, titles, phrases, names, or any other words, symbols or designations that are used herein are the property of their respective owners and are used for identification purposes only.

> FOR QUICK AND EASY COOKING TIPS LOOK OUT FOR OUR HACK ATTACKS!

CONTENTS

INTRODUCTIONS	05
APPETIZERS	09
SOUPS & SALADS	27
MAINS	55
VEGGIES & SIDES	125
DRESSINGS & SAUCES	149
DESSERTS & SWEETS	163
SNACKS	197
INDEX	230

IN GAME DOWNLOADS

- CHECK OUT THE IN GAME DOWNLOADS TOO — IDEAS HOW YOU CAN MAKE THE RECIPES YOUR OWN!

CLAUDIA'S INTRO: MY SECRET LIFE AS A VOICE-ACTING FOOD HACKER

I've been a working actress in Hollywood since I landed my first NBC series at eighteen and many people know me as Commander Susan Ivanova in the sci-fi series Babylon 5. I also have a career as a voice actress and have been featured in over twenty-five video games, including Warcraft, The Elder Scrolls V: Skyrim, Fallout, Halo and Call of Duty, (for a complete list see p.44) but I've got a secret life only my friends and family know about—I'm a serious cook.

I study cookbooks, experiment with famous recipes, have a fully fitted-out kitchen but because I'm also busy working on various TV series and computer games as a voice actor plus running my non-profit; I've had to develop workarounds and tricks to make fast, easy and delicious snacks and meals on the run. In fact, hacking foods is something I've been doing since I was a teenager.

My first—I took a nearly empty Dijon mustard jar that had a little mustard clinging to its sides and figured out that if I put vinegar and a pinch of salt in the jar, shook it up, added olive oil and shook again, I would have a perfect vinaigrette for salad, asparagus, beans, even fish! Next, add some minced garlic or shallots, some fresh herbs or even a tiny bit of lemon juice or anchovy paste to the dressing and I never needed to buy salad dressing again (plus no chemicals or dodgy ingredients).

Fish is another favorite hack. How to make sure you never make the common mistake of over-cooking your fish: pre-heat an oven to 400° then pop your fish in and turn the oven off. When you come back 10-20 minutes later (depending on the thickness of the fish) your fish is moist and delicious not dry and overcooked.

Heck, I have so many hacks to share, I can't even get through this introduction without wanting to get you started.

Take hard-boiled eggs. People mess that up all the time. A dark ring around the yolk or difficulty in peeling the shell is a sign they were not cooked correctly. Hack solution: Simply put eggs in a pot, cover with cold water and bring to a boil. Then turn the heat off and stick a lid on the pot. After 10-13 minutes remove the lid and put the pot of eggs under cold running water until the water is cool. Voila! You now have a perfectly cooked egg with no gray ring.

Here's a sandwich hack for when I need a quick protein fix but don't want to eat bread or mayonnaise: take a big iceberg lettuce leaf and lay some turkey slices in it, a few slices of avocado and a smear of mustard or a sliced pickle for an acidic flavor and there you have it—a healthy wrap. It takes about ten seconds to make but is nutritious and low in fat and calories, you can also eat it with one hand while gaming!

One pan wonder healthy breakfast hack: put a little water in the bottom of the pan then squish a bunch of spinach or baby kale on top of the water; crack a couple of eggs on top of the spinach and place a lid on the pan; then slowly steam everything, so you have steamed greens and poached eggs. Top with a drizzle of lemon olive oil and crunchy sea salt and man, what a delicious way to start the day. You can even top it with your favorite cheese or some roasted nuts.

Mark and I have been pen pals for quite some time now, he sends me lovely flower photos and we chat about life, the universe and everything. He's a long-time gamer and I have a long career working as a voice actor on computer games so a book with recipes for gamers, coders and anyone who spends a lot of time with their computer seemed to be something we were destined to write.

I've also included some of my food adventures in Hollywood, and stories and recipes contributed by my wonderful friends in the industry.

Learn these hacks and go-to recipes and you'll never have to face the vicious dilemma between your appetite and the happiness that comes from gaming or getting your code to work.

— *Claudia Christian*

MARK'S INTRO: GAME AND COOK

Gamers are a unique breed. We have our own language and our own rules of online engagement. We also have our own likes and dislikes, food-wise. If you asked the non-gaming public what gamers eat you'd get clichéd answers—cheese puffs, M&Ms, six packs of caffeine-laden soda. While it is true gamers enjoy food that is easily eaten with one hand, we are also possessed of taste buds and enjoy delicious food. That was one of the main reasons I decided to write this book with Claudia—to share easy, fast and delicious recipes with gamers like myself. A quick search revealed a mere handful of cookbooks for gamers, but they didn't look to be written by anyone who was actually into the gaming scene, either as a gamer or someone who worked in the video game industry.

Claudia has voiced some iconic game character voices over the years, and for some pretty major franchises: World of Warcraft, Fallout 4, and Call of Duty to name but a few. I've been a gamer since the 1970s on the original big three game systems; the Atari 2600, Mattel Intellivision and Coleco's Colecovision. In the years since, I've continued gaming, maintaining my own collection.

I got my start cooking as most of us do, with my mother. She was a wonderful woman and an amazing cook. It didn't matter what ingredients she had on-hand, she could make wonderful meals for our family of five kids. It wasn't until I moved out of home that I began my own culinary experimentation. One of the first recipes I learned to cook on my own is a quick chicken parmesan, using pre-made breaded chicken patties, some sauce from a jar and some shredded cheese. Not exactly 5-star fine dining, but definitely gamer-approved! We had to think about the look of the book and decided on 8 BIT style graphics. There's lots of ways to represent gaming but I started out as an old school gamer, right at the beginning in the 70s, so that felt right.

So here's Snack Hacks! We hope it brings an extra touch of speedy deliciousness to your gaming.

— *Mark Michel*

APPETIZERS

"An appetizer is traditionally used to stimulate one's appetite for what's to come but sometimes I like to make a whole meal of tasty little bites and skip the main course!"

TOTALLY LOCO MINI TACO BOWLS

In Total Overdose, you play Ramiro Cruz, the criminal brother of DEA agent Tommy Cruz, on the hunt to take out a Mexican drug gang. You have a nice selection of weaponry at your disposal and a series of loco movies to take out the garbage but one move they won't see coming is the power up you get from a batch of these small taco bowls. Alternatively, you can use them as improvised ninja stars.

Inspired by the video game Total Overdose

0:04 PREP TIME

0:10 COOK TIME

2-4 SERVINGS

INGREDIENTS

- 1 lb lean ground beef
- 2 Tbsp taco seasoning mix
- 4 soft corn tortilla shells (6-inch size)
- 1 cup cheddar cheese (or your favorite cheese)

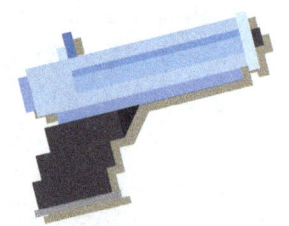

METHOD

1. Preheat oven to 400°. Take tortillas and place between two damp paper towels and microwave for 45 seconds until tortillas are pliable.

2. For bite-size taco bowls, use a biscuit cutter to create smaller tortillas from the larger ones. Spray plate with cooking spray and run the tortillas over the plate on both sides, then place the tortillas in between the spaces of the muffin tins to form a small bowl with the tortillas (see hack on page 12).

3. Brown ground beef, adding in taco seasoning as you cook meat. Remove beef with a slotted spoon, so there is no grease in the meat and hold in a separate bowl.

4. Pre-bake tortillas for 10 minutes, then remove and fill with a teaspoon of the meat.

5. Top with a pinch of shredded lettuce and your favorite shredded cheese. Repeat until all the tortillas are filled. Serve with sour cream or salsa.

IN GAME DOWNLOADS

- TRY USING GROUND CHICKEN OR PORK FOR A DIFFERENT FLAVOR.
- IF YOU'RE VEGAN, SUBSTITUTE THE MEAT WITH YOUR FAVORITE BEAN.
- YOU CAN ALSO SUBSTITUTE TACO SEASONING WITH OTHER SEASONINGS LIKE CHILI POWDER.

HACK ATTACK!

MUFFIN TIN TACO HACK

We've almost all used muffin tins to make cupcakes or cornbread muffins at one time or another. But the muffin tin isn't just for making cakes!

Try flipping the muffin tin over and spraying the backside with a little cooking spray. Then gently nestle a corn or flour tortilla in between 4 of the protruding cups. Bake the tortilla in an oven that's been pre-heated to 400° for approximately 10 minutes. The result is an edible taco bowl.

You can even make traditional taco shells using the upside-down muffin tin by sliding a full-sized tortilla between 2 of the protruding cups and forming it into a "U" shape. Bake at 400° for 10 minutes and then fill with your favorite taco fillings!

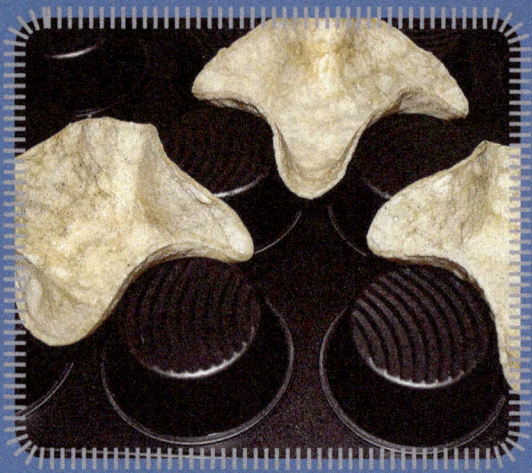

WARHOG BACON-WRAPPED PINEAPPLE BITES

Those silly hogs are at it again! They've got their drab-green garb on and are battling each other, and it's all-out war for these trotter-hoofed pigs! Fortunately you are far from the action, but you can enjoy a sweet pork taste with these bacon-wrapped pineapples and follow all the action on the battlefield, at least until it's your turn to make a move! You and 4 of your gaming buddies can enjoy this one.

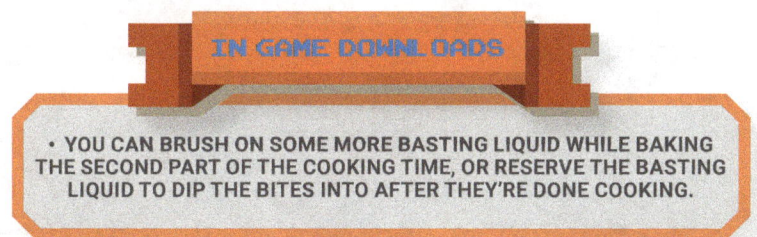

IN GAME DOWNLOADS

- YOU CAN BRUSH ON SOME MORE BASTING LIQUID WHILE BAKING THE SECOND PART OF THE COOKING TIME, OR RESERVE THE BASTING LIQUID TO DIP THE BITES INTO AFTER THEY'RE DONE COOKING.

INGREDIENTS

FOR PINEAPPLE BITES:
1 pineapple diced (or canned pineapple, drained)
½ lb uncooked bacon cut in half
Toothpicks

FOR BASTE:
2 drops liquid smoke
1 Tbsp hot sauce
1 Tbsp mustard
1 Tbsp honey

METHOD

1. Pre-heat oven to 450°. Spray wire rack with non-stick spray and place over a lined baking sheet.

2. Wrap half a slice of bacon around pineapple and put onto the wire rack. Bake in oven for 20 minutes.

3. While pineapples are cooking, put liquid smoke, hot sauce, mustard and honey into a small mixing bowl and whisk together into a basting liquid.

4. After 20 minutes, take bacon-wrapped pineapples out of oven and brush with basting liquid, then return to oven for another 5-10 minutes.

Inspired by the game Hogs of War for the Playstation

BRICKY NACHOS

You have been working on a specific map for Minecraft for what seems like days – or at least "Minecraft Days" – and you've managed to locate a village and planted yourself there so you can begin the task of obtaining the necessary ingredients and supplies to build the Nether Gate and strong armor, but so far you've only managed to dig up some iron ore. It seems you may have to dig further in order to locate the precious and elusive diamond ore. While you're digging in the game, you can dig deep with this gamer favorite multi-layered nacho dish that will have you mining all day. You and your Minecraft building friends will enjoy digging down to bedrock with this recipe to find delicious cheesy gold!

Inspired by the game Minecraft

0:10 PREP TIME

0:25 COOK TIME

2-4 SERVINGS

INGREDIENTS

1 bag of tortilla chips broken up, but not crushed
1 can (12 oz) refried beans
1 can (12 oz) black beans
2 cups mild or medium salsa
16 oz shredded cheese (cheddar or Monterey Jack)
8 oz sour cream
1–2 sprigs of chives, chopped

METHOD

1. In a microwave-safe bowl, heat up refried beans, at the same time drain black beans.

2. Once refried beans are heated to the point you can scoop them out with a spoon, begin layering a sprayed or greased casserole dish with chips, then black beans and cheese. Next layer is chips with refried beans and cheese, then repeat both layers until all beans and chips have been used up. Final layer is made up of 4 oz of sour cream and more shredded cheese.

3. Cook casserole in a pre-heated oven at 350° for about 20 to 25 minutes or until top layer of cheese is lightly golden brown and completely melted. Serve with a dollop of sour cream and chopped chives and enjoy.

4. For a spicier dish, you can add in ½ a jar (8 oz) of jalapeño, or banana peppers, chopped. Just add the peppers in between each layer. Best eaten immediately but will refrigerate for a couple of days for leftovers.

HAM & CHEESE PUFFBALL PIE

In Kirby's adventure, the cute little Kirby — a puffball of pink, goes around inhaling his enemies and spitting them out as stars to stop other enemies. He's trying to save his world from the evil enemy Nightmare, who wants to infect the world with bad dreams. It's up to you and Kirby to stop him before he is successful. But you will get hungry along the way, why not make some Ham & Cheese Puffball Pie to help keep you going? These treats are perfect to have on-the-go, when you and your gaming friends are heading to a convention. Grab a few for a quick and tasty breakfast or serve with a salad for lunch or dinner!

Inspired by the game Kirby's Adventure

0:15 PREP TIME

0:25 COOK TIME

8-10 SERVINGS

INGREDIENTS

- 2 sheets puff pastry defrosted and rolled into 10-inch squares
- 1–2 Tbsp Dijon mustard, regular or grainy
- 6 oz shredded Swiss cheese
- 4 oz good quality sliced ham (I use thinly sliced smoky Black Forest or a dry cured ham like Speck or Prosciutto)
- 1 tsp chopped thyme leaves
- 1 Tbsp olive oil
- ¼ tsp balsamic vinegar or sugar

METHOD

1. Preheat oven to 400°. Line a baking sheet with parchment paper.

2. Sauté the onions in a little olive oil on medium low until they are caramelized (about 8-12 minutes). Halfway through the cooking add the balsamic vinegar or sugar (both work) and the pinch of salt, stir frequently. Onions should be limp and cooked all the way through. Don't let them dry out and get too brown, if necessary you can add a tiny bit of water while they cook to keep them moist. Or you can just use store bought caramelized onion jam.

3. Roll the pastry out on a lightly floured surface so the two-pieces are the same size, about 10-inch squares works nicely.

4. Place one piece of puff pastry onto the baking sheet and spread with mustard, leaving a ½-inch border. Sprinkle half of the shredded cheese over the mustard. Layer ham slices over the cheese, followed by the caramelized onions, thyme, and remaining cheese.

IN GAME DOWNLOADS

- SUBSTITUTE CHEDDAR OR JACK CHEESES FOR THE SWISS CHEESE. OR USE A MIXTURE OF A FEW CHEESES.
- SUBSTITUTE YOUR FAVORITE MUSTARD FOR THE DIJON (LEEK MUSTARD OR HONEY MUSTARD WORKS WELL).
- MAKE IT VEGETARIAN WITH GOAT CHEESE AND OR PESTO AND THINLY SLICED GRILLED VEGGIES (MAKE SURE THE VEGGIES ARE NOT TOO WET!) OR TRY ROAST BEEF WITH HORSERADISH MIXED WITH A LITTLE SOUR CREAM (OR IF YOU'RE VEGAN, SUBSTITUTE THE MEAT WITH YOUR FAVORITE BEAN).

Pinch of salt
½ cup of thinly sliced onions or jar of caramelized onion jam
1 large egg
1 Tbsp milk
1 Tbsp chopped fresh parsley (optional)

5. In a small bowl, whisk together egg, milk, and parsley if using. Lightly brush the border of the puff pastry with the egg wash. Place the second square of puff pastry over the top and press the edges to seal.

6. Brush a ½-inch border on the top sheet of puff pastry with egg wash. Fold bottom edge of puff pastry over to create a crust of double thickness. Crimp edges with a fork.

7. Brush top of puff pastry with egg mixture. Cut four, 1-inch slits in the center of the pie with a small, sharp knife to allow steam to escape while baking.

8. Bake for 25 minutes, until puffed and golden. Let stand for 10 minutes before slicing into squares and serving.

CLAUDIA'S FOODIE CHILDHOOD

YOU cannot grow up in The Nutmeg State and not end up loving to bake and cook. Growing up in Westport, Connecticut near The Sound there was a fellow named "Pete the Boat" who would catch fish and gather shellfish. He'd sell them to my parents and other neighbors. He mostly caught the very oily and strong flavored blue fish, which my mother would serve, baked with mayonnaise. Sometimes my mother would cook up his delicious shellfish for dinner on the weekends.

> "MY VOICE-OVER CAREER REALLY WAS STARTED IN A DARK, MOLDY BASEMENT IN CONNECTICUT WITH MY THREE RAMBUNCTIOUS, HILARIOUS BROTHERS."

Lobster, clams and oysters were steamed and served with butter and lemon wedges and big hunks of crusty bread bought from the Italian grocer down the road. We had seafood steams and clam bakes on Compo Beach where we buried the shellfish, corn, potatoes, onions and huge artichokes in a big hole in the sand with hot coals on the bottom. You cover the whole lot with seaweed and drop cloths. Then we'd play on the beach and in the water for hours until we'd built up massive appetite before gathering round to feast on this New England delight. I have wonderful memories of my dad making us turn the crank on our old-fashioned ice cream maker, the kids would have contests to see who could stand on the huge blocks of ice the longest. I only won once. We would take the freshest of fruit in season; peaches, strawberries and blueberries, fresh cream from a local dairy farmer and we would make the best ice cream I've ever tasted. I suppose I was a pretty spoiled kid, food wise, but we took it for granted that everything was homemade. My mum is from Germany and half French so growing up I was introduced to all sorts of dishes my friends knew nothing about. We would eat landjaeger (smoky dried sausages) for snacks, sent from Germany by my Oma. Sauerbraten, which is incredibly tender beef in a delicious sauce, lots of red cabbage and potato dishes and my favorite—the time intensive rouladen, thinly sliced beef rolled up with mustard, onion, ham and pickle and cooked in yet another wonderful sauce. The potatoes are important in German cooking because they soak up the sauces.

I was the only kid in Connecticut to go to school with blood and tongue zugenblutwurst sandwiches or liverwurst on landbrot, a hearty brown bread I absolutely adore. No one would trade lunch with me, that's for sure! I grew up loving sauerkraut and mustard and German cold cuts and sausages. Weisswurst with German mustard and a huge portion of Alsatian style sauerkraut is still one of my favorite all-time meals. I also love picking up a sausage from street vendors in Germany, they never disappoint. Because my mother's family lived in Alsace Lorraine, I was also exposed to choucroute and tarte flambée which is a delicious tart made of thinly rolled out dough slathered in crème fraiche or fromage blanc, thinly sliced onions and lardons then baked until crispy. To die for!

During all of this eating and learning and tasting various dishes, our idea of a treat was being allowed to eat American food. Kentucky Fried Chicken, pizza and even (I am embarrassed to admit) a frozen faux Tex-mex meal was our idea of heaven. On our birthdays my brothers and I would be able to choose our meal and inevitably it would be junk.

We were incredibly lucky to have a mum who worked and still took the time to put great, fresh food on the table and a Dad who adored grilling and puttering around in the garden. My Dad's specialty was minute steaks—very thin, heavily marinated steaks he would get from a butcher in NYC where he worked sometimes, carried back on the train to Connecticut and marinated overnight in his salty, pungent secret sauce. They'd be grilled the next evening and served with a big salad and potatoes (baked or fried). It was a simple meal but we adored it.

My voice over career really was started in a dark, moldy basement in Connecticut with my three rambunctious, hilarious brothers

During this time in my childhood I began performing. I started doing theatre at school and my brothers and I had a basement "radio station" where we would record Monty Python routines and improvised comedy shows. My oldest brother, Patrick, had a little tape recorder and he would record our shows so we had to be on top form. My love of doing voices, accents and characters was developed in these hours long sessions. If I could have a little wish come true, those tapes would arrive on my doorstep so I could listen to them and laugh again.

Decades later, when my theatrical agent suggested I start going up for voice over gigs I was totally confident—this was my comfort zone! That ability to improvise and create a character and voice out of a one-line description in a game, e.g., female pirate in England, helped me forge my voice over career. There's something very calming about being in the booth by myself and creating a voice for a game. I love the intense concentration it takes to pick up the lines and give two or three very different readings so the director has choices. You have to remember that we very rarely work with other actors and we don't know what the other actors sound like so you're part relying on experience and intuition and part pissing in the wind.

All in all, I have been blessed that I've been able to play-act for a living for my whole career! The fact that I can also indulge in my other passion, cooking, is like icing on an already delicious cake!

WITH MY FAMILY, THAT'S ME IN THE BOTTOM RIGHT

DRAGON KICKERS CHICKEN

While you're making your way through wave after wave of bad ass martial art thugs in the game Godhand, you're going to need a free hand in order to choose a godhand move from your roulette wheel. An order of dragonkickers chicken will give you enough of a boost to roundhouse kick your opponent's jaw all the way to the Milky Way as well as being the perfect finger food. This makes enough for up to two hyperactive button mashers but can easily be increased to satisfy more of your gaming friends.

Inspired by the video game God Hand for the Playstation

3:10 PREP TIME

0:40 COOK TIME

1-2 SERVINGS

INGREDIENTS

- 1-2 boneless, skinless chicken breasts
- 1 cup buttermilk
- 2 cups Italian seasoned breadcrumbs
- 2 Tbsp hot sauce (your favorite)
- 1 stalk celery, cut into strips

FOR DIP:
- 8 oz sour cream
- ¼ cup chives
- 2 tsp dill
- ¼ tsp pepper

METHOD

1. Soak chicken in 1 cup of buttermilk mixed with a couple dashes of hot sauce, and salt and pepper and place in refrigerator for approximately 2 hours.

2. Remove chicken and dredge in breadcrumbs. Make sure to pat down in bread crumbs to ensure breading sticks and coats completely on both sides. Place chicken on foil-lined baking tray and set in fridge for about an hour to allow breading to completely stick to chicken.

3. Preheat oven to 350°. Bake chicken for 40 minutes, flipping half way with a spatula.

4. While chicken is cooking, mix sour cream, chives, dill and pepper together in a bowl to make a dip.

5. When chicken is done, immediately place it into a large bowl and pour plenty of hot sauce on top then toss chicken until coated nicely. Serve with the dip.

IN GAME DOWNLOADS

- FOR SPICIER NUGGETS, USE HOTTER HOT SAUCE OR ADD HOT PEPPER FLAKES TO SAUCE MIX.
- FOR A DIFFERENT FLAVOR PROFILE, TRY SPRINKLING IN SOME TOASTED SESAME SEEDS OVER THE HOT SAUCE COVERED NUGGETS.

AMBIGRAM PALMIERS

You've been playing The Da Vinci Code video game for a few hours, trying to figure out the big mystery in the story. You've been from one end of the globe to the other, chasing down clues and solving intricate puzzles and now you're getting hungry for something just as tasty as the mystery! Try making some of these palmiers, and you can satisfy your taste for good food, and get a small taste of Paris as well!

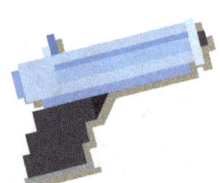

0:20 PREP TIME

0:30 COOK TIME

2-4 SERVINGS

INGREDIENTS

1 sheet of puff pastry
1 egg
TOPPINGS:
Parmesan and fresh black pepper
Chopped sun dried tomatoes and fresh basil
Goat cheese and lemon zest with fresh parsley
Finely chopped olives with minced garlic and fresh herbs
Pate or liverwurst with a thin layer of mustard and mincedcornichons
Blue cheese, finely chopped walnuts and apples
Blue cheese and bacon
Boat cheese and kalamata olives
Prosciutto slices with your favorite cheese
Sriracha sauce and minced chicken or veggies
BBQ sauce and minced pork

METHOD

1. Pre heat your oven to 400°. Lightly flour a surface and roll out the pastry dough lightly, just to get rid of the creases.

2. Crack the egg in a small bowl and beat it with a fork. Brush egg over surface of pastry dough then sprinkle your topping. There are limitless options, just keep the layers of ingredients thin.

3. Fold both long ends of the rectangle towards the middle to meet but do not over lap. Then do the same with those ends so you are making a log, press a bit so the sides crimp together just a little. Apply egg wash again on the exposed dough.

4. Turn the seam so it's facing away from you, trim the ends and cut in half-inch slices, place on a parchment lined baking sheet about 2 inches apart then chill them for about 10 minutes.

5. Bake for 10 minutes at 400° then lower oven to 350° and bake for another 20 or so minutes until they are golden brown and nicely puffed up. Cool before serving.

Inspired by The Da Vinci Code PC Video Game

HACK ATTACK!

FAKING FANCY PUFF PASTRY 1.0

Puff pastry is a pain in the butt to make by hand, trust me I've tried it. The store bought kind is fine. You can make loads of different delicious puff pastry appetizers, like my Ham & Cheese Puffball Pie (p.16). Check out the sweet ones too (p.176)! All you have to do is thaw it in the fridge and use your imagination.

HACK #1: How about the top for a chicken potpie? Easy, use puff pastry and just cut mini circles or one big circle and place on top of the pie filling. Then bake until puffy and golden.

HACK #2: Don't have any pizza dough but do have a hankering for pizza? Just thaw the sheet of puff pastry and place on a piece of parchment, fold the sides into edges and add your favorite sauce and toppings. Bake at 400° for about 15 minutes.

HACK #3: You can also cut the sheet onto two long slices and make two pizzas with no edge, just make sure you leave about an inch free of sauce and filling around the perimeter of the dough. If using raw meat or vegetables make sure you sauté the ingredients and cook them before putting on the pizza.

BACONATOR

While you're making your bacon-wrapped pineapple bites (p.13), why not try these bacon hacks!

HACK #1: If you want to chop bacon, stick it in the freezer for 5-10 minutes first then chop it up, much easier than slippery raw bacon!

HACK #2: If you are making bacon on the stove top and have a splatter guard you can keep the bacon you've already cooked by placing it on the splatter guard while cooking the next batch.

HACK #3: Put bacon on a cookie sheet and bake at 425° for 8-12 minutes flipping once, remove when it's brown but watch it so it doesn't burn. Drizzle a little maple syrup on each piece for a smokey, sticky, sweet treat!

STEALTHY MOUSE CHEESE PUFFS

Spy Mouse is a game that puts you in the tiny shoes of Agent Squeak – a mouse who is trying to keep away from mice-chasing cats, while at the same time trying his best to keep his cheese safe. Every mouse loves cheese, and these treats are perfect for company or just for you! These delicious, fast and easy cheese puffs will bring out the cheese-stealing spy mouse in all of us! They're also perfect for making ahead of your big convention road trip.

Inspired by the video game Spy Mouse

0:05 PREP TIME

0:10 COOK TIME

6-12 SERVINGS

INGREDIENTS

1 cup whole milk
1 stick butter
1 cup flour
4 eggs
1 cup shredded Gruyere cheese
⅓ cup grated Parmesan cheese
Salt and pepper, to taste

METHOD

1. Pre heat oven to 425°.

2. Bring milk and butter to a gentle boil then add the flour and reduce to medium heat, stir for a minute or two.

3. Let cool for a couple of minutes then place mixture in a food processor and, while it's running, add the eggs and cheeses and a little salt and pepper (salt is optional since the cheese is salty).

4. Cut a small corner off of a large ziplock plastic bag and add the mixture to bag so you now have a squeeze bag. Squeeze little triangles, about 2-3 inches long onto a non-stick baking sheet.

5. Sprinkle a little parmesan on each triangle. Bake for 10 minutes but keep your eye on them so they don't burn!! Serve hot or warm.

AT THE CONTROLLER'S BOOTH IN THE RECORDING STUDIO.

DINNER WITH FRIENDS MAKES LIFE WORTH LIVING. WITH PAT TALLMAN (LYTA ALEXANDER FROM BABYLON 5) AND MIRA FURLAN (DELENN FROM BABLYON 5) *(ABOVE)* AND YVETTE NELSON *(LEFT)*.

Soups & Salads

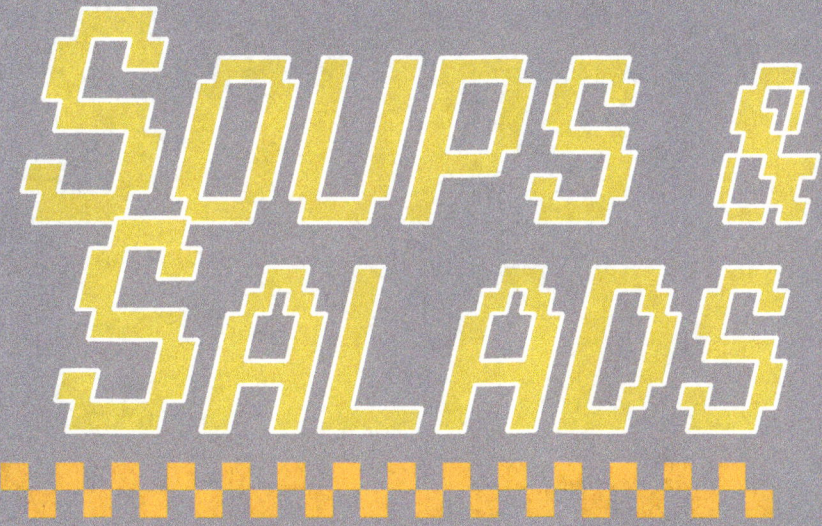

"A fast and healthy accompaniment to lunch or dinner, or as a meal in their own right!"

GARDEN WAR TOMATO-BASIL SOUP

It's all-out war between the plants and zombies, as you try to prevent the zombies from destroying your beautiful garden and reaching your safe home in order to feast on your tasty noggin meat. There doesn't seem to be a way to stop the hoards – but then again, no one has ever attempted to serve them a nice hot bowl of this tasty soup. This is an easy and quick-to-make soup and might just be the secret weapon you've been looking for to quell the advancing masses of zombies and put an end to the horrible war in the garden!

Inspired by the video game Plants vs. Zombies

0:05 PREP TIME

0:40 COOK TIME

4-6 SERVINGS

INGREDIENTS

4 cups canned whole tomatoes
4 cups tomato juice
12–14 washed fresh basil leaves
1 cup heavy cream
1 stick sweet unsalted butter
Salt to taste
¼ tsp cracked black pepper

METHOD

1. Combine tomatoes and juice in a saucepan. Simmer for 30 minutes.

2. Transfer liquid and tomatoes into a blender. Add basil leaves in small batches and puree.

3. Transfer mixture to saucepan and add in butter and cream. Add salt and pepper and continue to simmer until butter and cream are incorporated.

4. Garnish with fresh basil leaves and serve with a slice of your favorite bread.

HACK ATTACK!
CLAUDIA'S DAILY HACKS

Most of the people who know that I'm an avid and passionate cook, assume I must eat like a queen every day. Nothing could be further from the truth. So step into my kitchen and let me show you around. My weekday diet is essentially a series of food hacks and looks something like this:

BREAKFAST #1 around 6 am: a pot of Assam tea with low fat milk and maple syrup.

BREAKFAST #2 around 7 am, a hard-boiled egg with Dijon mustard smeared on it.

BREAKFAST #3 around 10 am: a leftover piece of chicken from dinner and a spoonful of vegan coconut "yogurt" (I know, chicken and vegan food, crazy!)

SNACK LUNCH at noon: a bag of organic spinach steamed with some lemon olive oil drizzled on it and some crunchy sea salt.

SNACK at 2 pm: a handful of raw walnuts.

SNACK DINNER at 4 pm: a piece of baked salmon with lemon juice and Yuzu hot sauce on it.

LATER DINNER: a bowl of organic beet and cabbage sauerkraut and an Icelandic yogurt or a frozen banana.

As you can see, I'm a grazer. I don't like sitting down for a meal unless I go for sushi or I'm cooking on the weekend. I LOVE fermented foods (hence the vegan yogurt and sauerkraut) and I enjoy making my own fermented veggies and yogurt. On the weekends my eating is far more conventional, and whoever I am with helps me test food (lucky boyfriend and besties!).

My weekend cooking is usually lunch and dinner or brunch and dinner. In the winter (Los Angeles doesn't actually have a winter, but we do have a rainy or occasional overcast-cooler season) I make hearty soups, stews and roasts or long and slow cooked meats.
In the summer I make fun salads for lunch with protein in them and grains and fresh or grilled vegetables. I make huge Nicoise salads with seafood or grilled whole branzino, garlicky spatchcocked chickens, endless inventive green salads with citrus or berries, nuts and whatever is fresh and wild, beet salads with goat cheese and lovely basil-filled Caprese salads to take advantage of the summer to-

matoes my friends grow. I love making eggs benedict or grain full blueberry pancakes and big platters of smoked salmon with all the fixings, bagels, herbed sour cream, sliced tomatoes and onions. And don't get me started on Heuvos rancheros with corn tortillas. I actually have a tortilla press!

> "As you can see, I'm a grazer. I don't like sitting down for a meal unless I go for sushi or I'm cooking on the weekend."

I love BBQing in the summer, grilled lamb chops with a Mediterranean inspired grilled zucchini and pepper dish with goat or feta cheese, some greens and maybe an orzo salad. I like leftovers, they provide take home care packages for friends and family and also breakfasts for me! I dive into experiments with molecular cuisine and ethnic dishes on the weekends. You will usually find me in the kitchen pretty much all weekend unless I am traveling. I have always been drawn to "clean" food. I don't make many sauces because I try to buy the best quality ingredients I can afford or find. I like to let the fish and meat or vegetable shine. I am perfectly happy with an avocado, dressed with fresh lime juice and Maldon salt for my lunch. I also make CC bowls a lot (see hack p.128). They can include a grain like barley, faro or lentils and some greens and maybe a can of tuna or leftover fish or chicken and a scoop of a fermented veggie topped with citrus or my homemade vinaigrette or hot sauce. Weird but really healthy and delicious!

I have learned from these cooking-centric weekends. I have had a few failures and a lot of successes. I read cookbooks as if they are novels, absorbing tips and ideas and then implementing them come Saturday morning. I hope that you find joy in cooking, after all we are feeding and nourishing our bodies and the people we love. Cooking is an expression of love to me, it's the way I show that I care for my friends and family. It is also a meditation for me, focusing on cooking takes away all of the day's worries and calms me; it is a miraculous balm for this overstimulated, uber-connected life we lead. I am an introverted extrovert by nature, meaning that I am inherently shy and uncomfortable at parties if I don't know anyone, but I love acting and I love cooking for people, an odd mix but hey, I have found my groove in life and accept myself the way I am. Cooking has brought me tremendous joy, a feeling of control and satisfaction as well as the knowledge that I can make other people or just myself, happy... and sated!

STUNT DRIVER'S CORN CHOWDER SOUP

In Split Second, you play a stunt driver on the set of a smash-hit fictional TV series called, "Split Second". In this game, you have to hit your "mark" at just the right moment to create a spectacular event in the "show". You have just caused a massive earthquake that has taken out a large suspension bridge and knocked out several of your racing competitors, and opened up a new driving route to boot! But now you are feeling a bit hungry and need something that is quick to make and hits the proverbial sweet spot in your stomach. Make some of this healthy and tasty corn chowder, and you will be back to finishing the game in no time!

0:10 PREP TIME

0:18 COOK TIME

2-4 SERVINGS

INGREDIENTS

1 medium onion chopped
1 Tbsp olive oil
2 cans (14½ oz each) chicken broth or 4 cups of homemade broth
3 large Yukon Gold potatoes cubed (you can peel if desired)
1 can (15¼ ounces) whole kernel corn, drained or 2 cups of fresh kernels
1 cup milk
Salt and pepper, to taste
⅓ cup all-purpose flour
Minced fresh parsley (optional)

METHOD

1. In a large saucepan, sauté onion in oil over medium heat, stirring occasionally until tender.

2. Add broth and potatoes and bring to a gentle boil.

3. Reduce heat; cover and simmer for 10-15 minutes or until potatoes are tender.

4. Stir in the corn, ½ cup of the milk, salt and pepper.

5. In a small bowl, whisk flour and remaining ½ cup of milk until smooth. Stir into soup; return to a boil.

6. Cook and stir for 2-3 minutes or until thickened.

7. Sprinkle with parsley if desired, and serve.

Inspired by the video game Split Second

IN GAME DOWNLOADS

- USE BACON FAT INSTEAD OF OLIVE OIL.
- ADD 2 CUPS OF CHOPPED HAM OR CHICKEN TO THE SOUP TO MAKE IT MORE HEARTY (YOU CAN ADD MORE CHICKEN BROTH IF DESIRED).
- ADD CRUMBLED BACON TO THE SOUP BEFORE SERVING.
- ADD FLAKED SALMON, CLAMS OR CRAB TO THE SOUP.
- ADD SOME TABASCO AND MINCED SCALLIONS FOR SPICE AND HEAT.

KING OF RED LIONS VEGGIE SOUP

Link is trying to rescue his sister from Ganon the evil sorcerer, who is also trying to get his hands on the sacred Triforce relic. Link's journey will take him far and wide through the land, including time sailing on his boat King of Red Lions! He will face many challenges before he locates his nemesis! If you're going to help Link on his long journey you'd better cook up a batch of veggie soup. A hearty soup that can be made ahead of time, or while you're playing if you use a slow-cooker. It makes enough for at least 4 people but freezes well for later adventures.

Inspired by the video game Legend of Zelda: The Wind Waker

0:10 PREP TIME

4:12 COOK TIME

4 SERVINGS

INGREDIENTS

1 large onion, sliced
2 celery ribs, sliced
1 cup corn
1 cup cooked baby potatoes, diced
2 cups fresh string beans
1 cup carrots, sliced
1 package bite-sized meatballs, parcooked
6 oz baby spinach
6 cups chicken broth
1 Tbsp salt
½ Tbsp pepper
2 dry bay leaves
½ Tbsp Italian seasoning

METHOD

1. Pre-heat oven to 350°. Cook meatballs for 12 minutes, remove from oven and let cool slightly.

2. While meatballs are cooking, slice veggies into uniform sizes and place into slow cooker along with spices.

3. Once meatballs have cooked, place them into slow cooker and add broth. Cook on low for 6 hours. If you want to have the soup sooner, simply dial the slow cooker to high and cook for 4 hours.

4. In the last hour, put spinach into slow cooker while removing bay leaves and cook for 1 hour until spinach wilts.

5. Serve with bread or crackers.

HOW TO ASSAULT THE DEATH STAR WHILE SIMULTANEOUSLY SNEAKING CIGARS

ONE of my fondest gaming memories involves my grandfather on my mom's side. We called him Pop-Pop, and he was a kindly, soft-spoken gentleman who loved three things: his grandchildren, his afternoon naps, and his occasional Phillips Cigar. My grandmother didn't like him smoking and so he came up with a rather ingenious way to sneak in his cigar and I was his willing accomplice.

When I was a kid, my family spent the summers in Brigantine, New Jersey. It was originally a sleepy, one-stoplight town but that changed with the arrival of the Brigantine Castle, an amusement pier built at the north end of town. So whenever my grandfather wanted a cigar he'd get me to pester him to go to the pier and then seem to give in and take me.

The showpiece of the amusement pier was a four story structure painted in a drab green that looked part Dracula's castle and part Soviet-era concrete fortress. It opened in 1976, along with other pier attractions such as a miniature golf course and gaming promenade that would allow people to play games of chance.

The carnival-type games were fun but it was the video game arcade that called to me. I would slip off my crutches and slide into the cockpit of the Star Wars game. It used wire-frame vector-graphics and had the original sounds from the movie. Pop-Pop would give me a stash of quarters to bury in the machine and, while I simulated Luke Skywalker's final X-wing fighter run on the Death Star, he'd sit on the pier and smoke to his heart's content.

Once he'd finished his cigar, he would come and collect me and bring me home – feeling pretty sure he'd put one over on my grandmother. But she was a very wise and astute woman and knew what Pop-Pop was doing all along, but she'd never voice her discontent, especially when we arrived home and she saw my beaming smile. She'd welcome us both back from our little excursion with a smile and some wonderful food she and my mother had made; either a bowl of her amazing vegetable soup (which is actually in this book, p.34) or perhaps, if I was lucky, some kielbasa and perogies!

Happy times!

> "AND WHILE I SIMULATED LUKE SKYWALKER'S FINAL X-WING FIGHTER RUN ON THE DEATH STAR, POP-POP WOULD GIVE ME A STASH OF QUARTERS TO BURY IN THE MACHINE AND THEN SIT ON THE PIER AND SMOKE TO HIS HEART'S CONTENT."

HACK ATTACK!

PICKLED ONIONS

I do not like raw onion in dishes, but sometimes onions work well so I make these easy pickled onions and keep them in the fridge to throw on salads, Mexican dishes, wraps, falafel, etc. They are very tasty on tostadas!

HACK #1: In a clean glass jar with a tightfitting lid, mix ½ cup of rice wine vinegar with 1 tablespoon of sugar, 1 teaspoon kosher salt and ½ cup hot water. Shake until sugar is dissolved. Bring a pot of water to boiling, and add one thinly sliced red onion. Let sit for just a few seconds in the hot water, then drain well and transfer onions to the jar with the vinegar. The pickled onions will be ready to use in about an hour or can be made ahead and kept in the fridge for up to a week.

HACK #2: Or you can just pour ½ cup of rice wine vinegar, ¼ cup of fresh lime juice, teaspoon of salt and a teaspoon of sugar over sliced red onions and let sit for about 20 minutes before using.

HACK #3: Or you can simply blanche the onions in boiling water then cool them and pat dry if you want a less aggressive onion smell and flavor, and less indigestion!

PLUMBER POWER GAZPACHO

Gaming's two favorite plumbers are at it again! But this time they're not cleaning out the sewer pipes or chasing down Donkey Kong. This time they're making their amazing gazpacho soup! Filled with plenty of fresh items from their garden, this refreshing and tasty soup will help cool you off while you're in a heated gaming session and put a triple jump back in your step. We guarantee no koopas were harmed in the making of this recipe!

0:05 PREP TIME

0:00 COOK TIME

1-2 SERVINGS

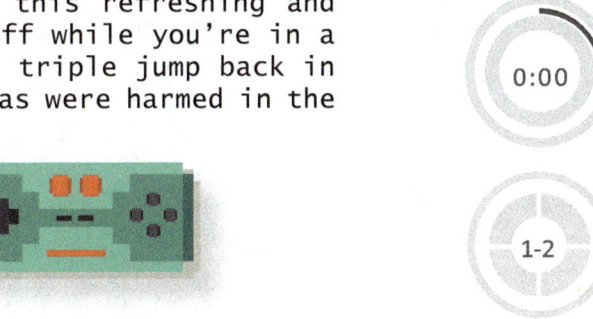

INGREDIENTS

¼ large cucumber
1 pint cherry tomatoes
1 large shallot
½ green pepper
1 tsp garlic powder
1 Tbsp salt
½ Tbsp pepper
4–5 dashes of hot pepper sauce (or more, depending on taste)

METHOD

1. Rough chop all vegetables and put into food processor or blender.

2. Add seasonings and blend until pureed well, adjusting seasonings if necessary. Serve and enjoy!

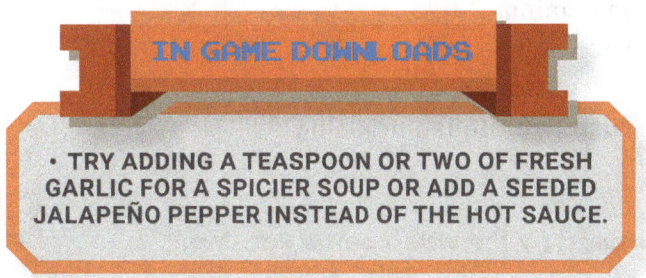

IN GAME DOWNLOADS

- TRY ADDING A TEASPOON OR TWO OF FRESH GARLIC FOR A SPICIER SOUP OR ADD A SEEDED JALAPEÑO PEPPER INSTEAD OF THE HOT SAUCE.

Inspired by the video game Mario Brothers

PELLET 3-BEAN SALAD

Pac-Man is forever racing through mazes attempting to gobble up all the pellets before the ghostly quartet is able to hunt him down. All he has to defeat the ghosts are his wits and super Pac-Pellets, which allow him to become the hunter. While you are busy attempting to get the high score in Pac-Man on your Atari 2600 or Xbox game system, try making a batch of this easy - and healthy side dish! It's almost as quick to make, as Pac-Man is at chomping pellets!

0:05 PREP TIME

0:00 COOK TIME

10 SERVINGS

INGREDIENTS

1 can (12 oz) blackbeans
1 can (12 oz) red kidney beans
1 can (12 oz) chick peas
1 medium green pepper, diced
½ onion, diced
1 Tbsp dried jalapeño/cilantro seasoning
1 Tbsp salt
½ Tbsp pepper
3 Tbsp light Italian dressing

Inspired by the video game Pac-Man

METHOD

1. Rinse all beans in a colander and let drain. Then put beans into a bowl along with chopped onions and green peppers.

2. Add salt, pepper, jalapeño/cilantro seasoning and dressing, then toss thoroughly until beans are all coated and mixed well.

3. Store in fridge until ready to serve. Makes approximately 10 cups of salad.

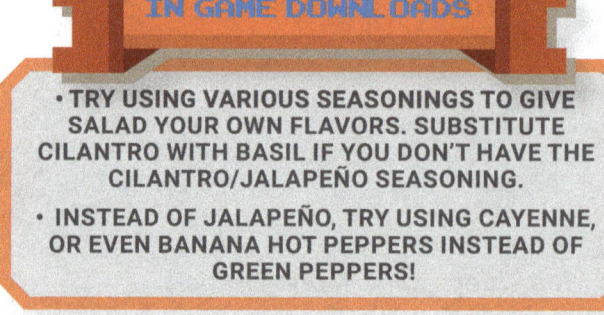

IN GAME DOWNLOADS

- TRY USING VARIOUS SEASONINGS TO GIVE SALAD YOUR OWN FLAVORS. SUBSTITUTE CILANTRO WITH BASIL IF YOU DON'T HAVE THE CILANTRO/JALAPEÑO SEASONING.
- INSTEAD OF JALAPEÑO, TRY USING CAYENNE, OR EVEN BANANA HOT PEPPERS INSTEAD OF GREEN PEPPERS!

FARM FRESH WATERMELON CUCUMBER SALAD

You have always wanted to be a farmer but have somehow found yourself working 9-5 as a web developer. But there is still a soft spot in your heart that yearns to get behind a tractor and work the land. Luckily you can still fulfil your fantasy by playing Farming Simluator 2019 – and while you're growing some yummy virtual veggies, why not make yourself some of this refreshing and tasty dish?

Inspired by the video game Farming Simulator

 0:05 PREP TIME

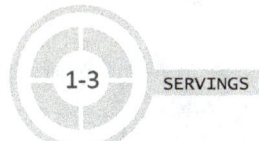 0:00 COOK TIME

1-3 SERVINGS

INGREDIENTS

FOR SALAD:

3 cups chilled seedless watermelon, cubed
1 cup chilled medium cucumber, chopped
1 cup crumbled feta cheese
½ cup red onion, thinly sliced
½ cup coarsely chopped mint
Fresh basil and/or parsley (optional)
Flaky sea salt and black pepper, to garnish

METHOD

1. Whisk the vinaigrette ingredients in a small bowl.

2. Combine the salad ingredients in a large bowl then toss with the vinaigrette and sprinkle a little flaky salt and black pepper on it, serve immediately.

FOR VINAIGRETTE:

¼ cup extra-virgin olive oil
2 Tbsp red wine vinegar
½ tsp kosher salt
Ground black pepper, to taste
Pinch of sugar

VOICE ACTOR PROFILE
CLAUDIA CHRISTIAN

GAMERS will identify Claudia as the voice of such video game characters as Aela the Huntress from The Elder Scrolls V: Skyrim, or Captain Maureen Ferran from Call of Duty: Infinite Warfare. She's also lent her voice talent to a myriad of other franchise video games such as World of Warcraft (Warlords of Draenor, Legion, and the upcoming installment – Battle for Azeroth).

Claudia's been acting for most of her life. Outside of games, she played Susan Ivanova in the sci-fi classic Babylon 5, but she's also appeared in such shows as NCIS, The Mentalist, and the Fox show 911 as Captain Maynard. She's worked with Morgan Freeman, Michael Keaton and Faye Dunaway, among others. While she continues to grace film and TV with her acting talent, she also runs a non-profit, The C3 Foundation, and has written several books—including Babylon Confidential and Wolf's Empire: Gladiator with Morgan Grant Buchanan, and The Original: The Trials of Sara Larkin.

IT LOOKS EASY BUT THERE ARE LOTS OF TAKES AND LOTS OF SCREAMING. SOMETIMES I LOSE MY VOICE AND IT TAKES DAYS TO RECOVER.

MARK: Can you give me an overview of the process of doing voice acting for video games?

CLAUDIA: You go to the studio and they hand you a big stack of lines and put you in the booth where you can see the director and the rest of the crew through a glass window. They speak to you through a microphone you can hear through your headset. Then you read a few takes of each line and sometimes the director asks you to try a number of different takes. You have to be very quick on your feet because you usually don't get to see the script beforehand. Being a good cold reader is an indication of your ability to do voice gigs.

MARK: Do you remember the first video game you auditioned for, and if you got the part?

CLAUDIA: In terms of auditions I can't recall, because you do so many, but I do know the first video game part I landed was Solar Eclipse. (For hard-core gamers, Solar

Eclipse was a video game released for the Sega Saturn system. Claudia voiced the character "Raven" Major Delany Kelt. Solar Eclipse came out in 1995 – around the same time Claudia's science fiction series Babylon 5 was in production.)

MARK: Can you talk about what goes into a video game voice assignment?

CLAUDIA: I either go to my agent (Abrams Artists) and do the audition in one of their booths with the director from the agency or I do the audition in my home studio and email it to my agent.

MARK: What was your favorite game to work on and why?

> "I WENT IN THINKING I WAS PLAYING A DRAGON AND GOT THERE ONLY TO FIND OUT I WAS A VERY ROUGH CHARACTER IN GRAND THEFT AUTO"

CLAUDIA: I love my character "Xal'atath; Blade of the Black Empire" in World of Warcraft because it reminded me of my role as Helga Sinclair in Disney's Atlantis when she turned on the "Jessica Rabbit" sexy voice.

MARK: What was the most difficult video game voice assignment you had?

CLAUDIA: Sometimes when I have a ton of dying scenes and fight scenes my voice poops out but apart from that I try to give my all to any of the games I appear in, an equal effort. But I can tell you the most awkward job was the time I was hired to do a voice in a "mystery" game. This is when you're not told what game you're working on, they even make up a fake title. The union rules have changed so they don't do that anymore. I went in thinking I was playing a dragon and got there only to find out I was a very rough character in Grand Theft Auto. At the time I was trying to pursue work in children's books and other more "PG" work, and it's hard now to convey how shocking the violence was in the GTA games was at the time. The rest of the entertainment industry was relatively tame, so I had my name removed from the final product. I just didn't want to be associated with really violent games... Of course as I got older I sort of relaxed about my 'holier than thou attitude' and realized that it's up to parents to control what they allow their kids to play.

MARK: When did you first decide to get involved in voice work?

CLAUDIA: My agent suggested I give it a shot because he thought I had a great voice.

MARK: Which is more difficult, voice acting or conventional acting?

CLAUDIA: Neither are "difficult" other than getting the work, now that's difficult, especially these days.

MARK: If you had your choice of voice gigs what would be your first choice?

CLAUDIA: Another animated feature film, preferably one that made a fortune, so I would get nice, fat residual checks and be able to grow my non-profit organization!

MARK: Would you like to see a company develop a game based on Babylon 5, and if so, would you be interested in reprising your role of Susan Ivanova?

CLING ON KLINGONS. GOT TO TRY SOME OF THOSE KLINGON RECIPES!

CLAUDIA: Sure, why not?

MARK: With all the various talents you have, would you be interested in developing a video game, and if so, what genre would it be?

CLAUDIA: Oh gosh, I'll leave that to the experts... if I ever did anything like that I would develop a game to teach kids how to cook. Aside from that I'm a huge reader of history. Something set in Medieval Europe with knights and swords and ladies that poison their enemies. You know, something nice.

MARK: Is there anything else you'd like to say to the gaming community?

CLAUDIA: I suppose my advice would be to have balance in your life. Play games but also engage with nature. Eat "fun food" but also "healthy food". Life is all about balance!

CLAUDIA'S GAMES!

HERE'S A LIST OF THE GAMES (AND A FEW VOICE ROLES) YOU CAN FIND ME IN. HAVE FUN PLAYING ANY YOU HAVEN'T COME ACROSS YET!

GODS AND HEROES (NETFLIX 2020) ROLE: HERA

LEAGUE OF LEGENDS (2019)

FALLOUT 76 (2018) ROLES: SHANNON RIVERS, MISS ANNIE, WILLIE MAE

CALL OF DUTY: INFINITE WARFARE (2016) ROLE: CAPTAIN MAUREEN FERRAN

WORLD OF WARCRAFT: LEGION (2016) ROLE: LADY LIADRIN

THE ELDER SCROLLS V: SKYRIM - SPECIAL EDITION (2016) ROLES: AELA THE HUNTRESS, LEGATE RIKKE, ADELAISA VENDICCI, ADRIANNE AVENICCI, BREYA, BRINA MERILIS, BRYLING, FALEEN, IONA, LAILA LAW-GIVER, POTEMA SEPTIM, RAYYA, SORLI THE BUILDER, UTHGERD THE UNBROKEN, VOLDSEA GIRYON, ZARIA

STARCRAFT II: NOVA COVERT OPS - MISSION PACK 3 (2016) ROLES: ROHANA & OTHER VOICE PARTS

BLADE KITTEN: EPISODE 2 (2015) ROLES: LEAD MAGASSE SISTER, GUARD POST, SQUAMATAN WORKER

DARKSIDERS II: DEATHINITIVE EDITION (2015)

FALLOUT 4 (2015) ROLES: DESDEMONA, MRS. WHITFIELD, MISTRESS MYSTERIOUS

HEROES OF THE STORM (2015)

STARCRAFT II: LEGACY OF THE VOID (2015) ROLE: ROHANA

DIABLO III: REAPER OF SOULS (2014)

WORLD OF WARCRAFT: WARLORDS OF DRAENOR (2014)

HEROES OF THE STORM LADY OF THORNS (2014)

DARKSIDERS II (2012) ROLE: MURIA

GUILD WARS 2 (2012) ROLES: MALA, PC NORN FEMALE

HALO 4 (2012)

THE ELDER SCROLLS V: SKYRIM (2011) ROLES: AELA THE HUNTRESS, LEGATE RIKKE, ADRIANNE AVENICCI, SORLI THE BUILDER AND WOLF-QUEEN POTEMA (& VARIOUS OTHER CHARACTERS)

BLADE KITTEN (2010) ROLES: LEAD MAGASSE SISTER, GUARD POST, SQUAMATAN WORKER

SHREK FOREVER AFTER: THE FINAL CHAPTER (2010)

PIZZA MORGANA: EPISODE 1 - MONSTERS AND MANIPULATI (2009) ROLE: ABBIE

GEPPETTO'S SECRET (2005) ROLE: BLUE FAIRY

SHREK 2 (2004) ROLES: GINGERBREAD MAN, PEASANT, LEPRECHAN

SHREK 2 (2004) ROLES: FAIRY GODMOTHER, FEMALE CITIZEN

SECRET WEAPONS OVER NORMANDY (2003) ROLE: WHITE ROSE

DISNEY'S ATLANTIS: THE LOST EMPIRE (GAME & MOVIE 2001) ROLE: HELGA SINCLAIR

EARTH & BEYOND (2002) ROLE: LADY KATHERINE ISABELLA OLIVIA DEWINTER

SUMMONER 2 (2002) ROLES: SANGARIL, LOGOSARCH, ROSALIND, DAMA HERAS

TITAN WARS (1995)

SOLAR ECLIPSE (1995) ROLE: "RAVEN" MAJ. DELANY KELT

SOMETIMES VOICE ACTRESS, SOMETIMES COOK, SOMETIMES STAR FUREY PILOT!

IVANOVA'S RUSSIAN BORSHT

Babylon 5 was the last of the Babylon space stations. 5-miles long and constructed of two million, five-hundred thousand tons of metal – Babylon 5 stood against the darkness and the light during the Shadow Wars. But in Babylon 5: Into the Fire, you are put onto the station as you control one of several playable characters (President John Sheridan, Michael Garibaldi, Delenn or Captain Lochley), who are in a struggle to hold the fragile alliance between the League of Non-Aligned Worlds and their increasing territorial squabbles. Of course, the one person who could definitely put an end to the league's squabbles would be Susan Ivanova – at this point in time, Captain of her own ship – but she's out on the rim on patrol with some Rangers. While you play the demo for this never-released game (there are downloads online), you can try some of Ivanova's Russian Borsht. "Boom today, boom tomorrow – there's ALWAYS a boom!"

0:10 PREP TIME

0:15 COOK TIME

6-8 SERVINGS

INGREDIENTS

2 cups shredded fresh beets
1 cup shredded carrots
1 cup finely chopped onion
2 cups water
½ tsp salt or to taste
Fresh ground pepper, to taste
2 cans (14½ oz each) beef or vegetable broth
1 cup finely shredded cabbage (green, red, savoy, any kind)
1 Tbsp lemon juice
Sour cream or cream fraiche
Chopped chives or fresh dill sprigs or if you can't find them then chop up some spring onions

METHOD

1. In a saucepan, bring the beets, carrots, onion, water and salt to a boil. Wear disposable gloves when grating the beets or grip the beet in some plastic wrap so you don't stain your hands. You can also use precooked beets or even canned in a pinch, just skip steps 1-2 and add them when you add the broth and cabbage at step 3.

2. Reduce heat; cover and simmer for 20 minutes.

3. Add broth, cabbage and butter; simmer, uncovered, for 15 minutes.

4. You can serve this soup hot, warm or cold. Just before serving, stir in lemon juice.

5. Top each serving with a dollop of cream fraiche or sour cream and chives or dill.

Inspired by the abandonware game Babylon 5: Into the Fire

DON'T MESS WITH IVANOVA, SHE'S DEATH INCARNATE

ON SET, BABYLON 5 DAYS WITH MY FANTASTIC FRIENDS. BILL MUMY, MIRA FURLAN, PAT TALLMAN,

"BOOM TODAY, BOOM TOMORROW—THERE'S ALWAYS A BOOM."

HOT, CRAMPED, I EVEN SAT THROUGH AN EARTHQUAKE IN ONE OF THESE COCKPITS BUT THE SHOW MUST GO ON BABY!

CHICKEN CHASER CHICKEN SALAD ROLL

While playing the game Fable, you realize the non-playable characters have begun calling you, "Chicken Chaser" as you pass by them. You aren't sure as to why, until you realize you've been chasing down chickens in the game and giving them a kick with your boot to get them to fly and cluck. Then you realize you're getting hungry and you want something quick and tasty to eat. Why not make some Chicken Chaser Salad, and satisfy your appetite for chicken while chasing chickens? This recipe makes enough for a week's worth of chicken salad for one gamer, and you can earn that first nick-name in the game Fable!

2:15 PREP TIME

0:00 COOK TIME

6-7 SERVINGS

INGREDIENTS

- 20 oz diced chicken, fresh cooked or canned
- ½ onion, diced
- ½ green pepper, diced
- 1 tsp ranch dressing
- 1 cup mayonnaise
- ½ cup brown mustard
- 2 splashes (approx. ¼ tsp) white vinegar
- ⅓ cup dried cranberries
- Salt and pepper, to taste

Inspired by the video game Fable

METHOD

1. In a bowl, flake chicken with a fork to consistency desired.

2. Mix in green peppers, onions, mayo, dressing, mustard and vinegar, then season with salt and pepper. Mix well until all ingredients are well tossed.

3. Place container in refrigerator for at least 2 hours to allow flavors to meld together.

4. Serve on Kaiser roll, toast or even crackers.

TRace-On CODE SLAW

In the game Tron: Maze-A-Tron, you are playing as Flynn – the plucky programmer who creates the program Tron (TRace-On, for those old-school programmers). But Flynn has been beamed into the world of the computer and has to help Tron stop the Master Computer from absorbing every program in the world. In this game, Flynn must traverse various mazes in order to free programs. Flynn might not need actual food while he's in the game, but you will! Make a batch of this refreshing coleslaw, so you can get back to the game and save the computer world!

2:10 PREP TIME

0:00 COOK TIME

2-4 SERVINGS

INGREDIENTS

1 head of cabbage, washed and dried well
2 large carrots
1 cup mayonnaise
1 Tbsp sugar
1 tsp Dijon mustard
2 Tbsp white vinegar
2 tsp black pepper
Salt, to taste

METHOD

1. Shred cabbage pretty fine, shred carrots to same consistency and put into a large mixing bowl.

2. Put mayonnaise, sugar, mustard, vinegar and pepper into bowl and mix all ingredients well until all cabbage and carrots are coated in mixture.

3. Refrigerate for at least 2 hours before serving—overnight is best to allow coleslaw to develop a deeper, richer flavor.

4. Serve as a side dish with your favorite meal.

Inspired by Maze-A-Tron for the Intellivision game system

IN GAME DOWNLOADS

- TRY USING DIFFERENT COLORED CABBAGE FOR A MORE COLORFUL SLAW OR ADD SOME ONIONS OR GREEN PEPPERS FOR ADDED FLAVOR!
- THIS RECIPE CAN ALSO BE MADE WITH GRAINY MUSTARD OR EVEN MUSTARD POWDER.
- YOU CAN ALSO ADD RAISINS OR SEEDS OR NUTS TO COLESLAW.
- I LOVE ADDING A SWEET AND WARM SPICE ELEMENT TO SLAW LIKE INDIAN SPICES OR JUST A PINCH OF CINNAMON AND SOME GOLDEN RAISINS, GREEN ONION AND CILANTRO, TASTES TOTALLY UNIQUE.

CC'S SOUTHWEST GRILLED CORN & BLACK BEAN BUCKSHOT SALAD

I love this simple but tasty salad with grilled chicken, fish or on its own in a cold iceberg lettuce cup. It makes a fun side or main dish. A western themed dish needs a western themed game. How about the Xbox game Gun? Colton White has been done wrong by some low-down cowpoke and is out on a mission of revenge. He has only his steady steed, his trusty gun, and now a grilled corn and black bean salad to aid him along the way.

Inspired by the video game Gun for the original Xbox

PREP TIME 0:15
COOK TIME 0:07
SERVINGS 2-4

INGREDIENTS

- ½ cup lime juice
- 1 tsp of red wine or balsamic vinegar
- 6 Tbsp olive oil
- ½–1 tsp chili powder (to preference)
- ½ tsp cumin powder
- Hot sauce to taste (I like the jalapeño Tabasco for this dish)
- 1 tsp sugar, honey or maple syrup (optional but balances the acid in the dressing)
- 2 cups corn, fresh or frozen
- 1 can (15 oz) black beans, rinsed and drained

METHOD

1. To make the salad dressing, combine the lime juice, vinegar, olive oil, chili powder, cumin powder, hot sauce, sweetener of choice and salt and pepper to taste in a small bowl. Mix until sugar is dissolved, if using.

2. Prepare the vegetables: To grill the corn and peppers, heat a grill to high, spray the corn and peppers with olive oil spray or rub some oil on them then put the corn and peppers on the grill turning every few minutes until they are nicely roasted and some kernels start to make popping noises on the corn. The peppers should look blistered but not completely black. If you overcook or burn the peppers just peel them before chopping (let them cool off first!). To roast the corn and peppers, heat a skillet (a cast iron pan does a terrific job) with 1-teaspoon oil. Add corn, peppers and a big pinch of salt and pepper and let roast on medium high heat for 5 - 7 minutes until corn starts to darken in color and peppers soften. Let cool a bit before chopping into large dice (**see safety note). Remove kernels from corn using a sharp knife.

- 1 can (15 oz) garbanzo beans (or you can use 2 cans of black beans or even one each of black and kidney or navy beans)
- 1 grilled or roasted orange, red, or green bell pepper diced (optional)
- 1 cup tomatoes, diced with seeds removed
- ½ cup red, green or sweet Maui onion, diced
- 1 grilled or roasted jalapeño, diced with seeds removed
- 1–2 avocados, diced
- ¼ cup cilantro, chopped
- Salt and pepper, to taste

3. Place peppers and corn in a large bowl, add beans, tomatoes, onions, chopped avocado and cilantro. Drizzle the salad dressing over the top. Mix the salad gently until the dressing is evenly dispersed. Taste again and make sure it has enough dressing and salt and pepper, lime juice and hot sauce. Serve immediately or chill in the refrigerator for 1 - 2 hours prior to serving.

"*P*UT THE CORN AND PEPPERS ON THE GRILL TURNING EVERY FEW MINUTES UNTIL THEY ARE NICELY ROASTED AND SOME KERNELS START TO MAKE POPPING NOISES ON THE CORN "

** Safety note: When chopping any hot pepper like the Jalapeño, wear disposable gloves when seeding the pepper. If you love spice you can leave the seeds in; if you like a more mellow heat, slice chili down the middle and scrape the seeds out with a sharp knife, then dispose of seeds.

MAINS

"Whether you have 15 minutes or 45 minutes to prepare a meal, you'll find something here to satisfy everyone!"

BEST OF SHOW WATCH PARTY CHILI

Couldn't attend E3, but are planning to watch it on your favorite console's streaming service? You and your friends will love my watch party chili recipe. It can be prepped and put into a crock pot several hours before your party. Serve it up with a side of tortilla chips or some Bricky Nachos (p.56), and your gaming friends will vote you Best in Show!

0:10 PREP TIME

4:00 COOK TIME

6 SERVINGS

INGREDIENTS

- 1 large onion, chopped
- 2 Tbsp minced garlic
- 1 large green pepper, diced
- 1 pack of your favorite bratwurst or hot dogs, diced
- 2–3 Tbsp chili powder
- 1–1½ Tbsp paprika
- 1–1½ Tbsp ground cumin
- 1–2 Tbsp crushed pepper flakes
- 2 cans (8 oz each) black beans, rinsed and drained
- 1 can (8 oz) red or white beans, rinsed and drained
- 4 oz diced banana hot peppers and some banana hot pepper liquid

METHOD

1. Toss everything in a crock-pot and cook for 4 hours on high or 8 hours on low. Occasionally stir to ensure everything mixes well. You can also let it cook longer, for a deeper, richer flavor – just like regularly-cooked chili.

2. You can serve with tortilla chips or top with cheese and a dollop of sour cream and chives for garnishing.
This recipe easily doubles, too! Great to serve to friends.

Inspired by the E3 Electronic Expo video game convention

IN GAME DOWNLOADS

- BRATWURST AND HOT DOGS CAN BE SUBSTITUTED WITH ANY TYPE OF MEAT. JUST BROWN AND DRAIN THE MEAT IN A PAN ON YOUR STOVE BEFORE ADDING IT TO THE CHILI.
- YOU CAN SUBSTITUTE 1-2 CANS OF DICED CHILI PEPPERS FOR THE BANANA PEPPERS.
- FOR A HOTTER CHILI, SIMPLY ADD MORE CRUSHED PEPPER FLAKES OR REPLACE BANANA HOT PEPPERS WITH DICED JALAPEÑO PEPPERS, OR EVEN ADD SOME HOT SAUCE!

SKILLS FOR KILLS GRILLED SKIRT STEAK

What does every good agent in Crackdown need to get stronger? Sure, steroids are one thing, wanting to kick criminal butt another, but if you're going to save the city from drug lords, gangs and whatever the heck that thing with four arms is then you need delicious protein and lots of it! This grilled skirt steak is perfect for keeping you climbing buildings as you chase down that last agility orb. Hey! I can see my house from up here! This recipe's good for up to eight hungry agents.

1:00 PREP TIME

0:15 COOK TIME

8 SERVINGS

INGREDIENTS

2 lb of skirt steak
¼ cup steak or rib rub

FOR MARINADE:
¼ cup olive oil
1 Tbsp of salt
1 tsp black pepper
3 cloves minced garlic
½ cup orange juice
½ cup lime and/or lemon juice
1 Tbsp Worcestershire sauce
1 minced jalapeño or 1 Tbsp hot sauce

METHOD

1. Mix marinade ingredients in a blender, food processer or bowl, pour over steak and put in fridge for about 2 hours.

2. Remove from marinade and sprinkle on rub, let sit for 30 minutes.

3. Heat grill to high (about 450°) and cook steak for a 2-5 minutes on each side depending on desired doneness and thickness of meat.

4. Let meat rest for 10 minutes before slicing across the grain rather than parallel with it. Cutting across the fibers of the meat makes it easier to chew so make sure you do this correctly.

The corn and black bean salad (p.52) goes great with this dish!

Inspired by the video game series Crackdown

HACK ATTACK!
HACKY PARCHMENT PAPER

Want to stop your food sticking to the pan AND save time washing up? Parchment paper is the answer!

Parchment paper is a wonderful non-stick tool to have in your kitchen drawer where you keep the tin foil and plastic wrap. It can be purchased in most any supermarket in the same section where you find food storage bags, tin foil, kitchen wrap, etc. In the UK and Australia parchment paper is sometimes called bakery paper or baking paper.

Parchment differs from wax paper as it is grease proof. It will burn at very high temperatures (over 450°) but that doesn't prohibit it from being used for pizzas at 500° which I have done, it might get scorched but it has never flamed up on me. That said, do NOT use wax paper for baking, etc. as it is flammable and will leave a residue on your edibles.

There is no right or wrong side of parchment paper and it comes either in a roll or in individual pre-cut sheets, which are terrific for baking sheets.

I use parchment to line my baking sheets for everything from cookies to fish, it makes for a clean and easy surface to work on and the food doesn't stick.

Parchment paper is made from paper pulp which is run through a bath of sulfuric acid or zinc chloride for you science nuts!

SURVIVING CRYOSTASIS SPAGHETTI

You've just come out of cryostasis and you've got to search the Commonwealth for your kidnapped child, but spending so long on the ice has left you cold and beset by a grumbling stomach that just won't quit. Before you can save anyone you first have to save your appetite!

Inspired by the video game Fallout 4

0:02 PREP TIME

0:25 COOK TIME

1 SERVINGS

INGREDIENTS

1 package of Ramen noodles minus flavor packet
5 mini frozen meatballs
1 cup spaghetti sauce
Parmesan cheese

METHOD

1. Preheat oven to 350°. Bake meatballs 20-25 minutes.

2. In the meantime, pour 3 cups of water into a microwave-safe bowl and heat for 4 minutes. Place 1 whole package of Ramen noodles (unbroken) into water and cover. Let noodles soak until al dente. Strain fully-prepared noodles.

3. Plate some noodles onto a plate, pour some tomato sauce on top and place cooked meatballs on top of sauce. Place into microwave for 3 minutes to heat sauce.

4. Top meal with Parmesan cheese and serve.

Recipe is easily doubled to cook for two!

PRO GAMER PROFILE

WESTBALLZ

WHEN I started writing this book I thought I'd ask some of my friends involved with computer gaming and voice acting to share their perspectives on gaming and cooking and offer up a few recipes. Fortunately, I didn't have to look very far for a pro gamer because my cousin Weston Dennis (Westballz) is a professional Super Mario Smash Bros. gamer. His bio speaks for itself: Westballz is a member of G2 Esports team and is currently ranked 2nd and 7th on the SoCal Melee and Project M Power Rankings, respectively, and 8th on the 2015 SSBMRank.

CLAUDIA: What do you do for nutrition when you're playing a really long tournament? Any favorite gaming foods or quick energy meals you turn to?

WESTBALLZ: I try to have a big breakfast, usually eggs, toast, and meat, then during the tournament I like to eat fruits that are high in sugar, so I can maintain focus.

CLAUDIA: What was the first video game you ever played, and what did you like about it?

WESTBALLZ: My first video game was Mario Kart for the Super Nintendo. It felt rewarding to be able to progress through the game and get better and beat harder levels every time.

CLAUDIA: Who is your favorite video game character and why?

WESTBALLZ: My first video game character, Mario. He just had a sense of humor most other characters did not have.

CLAUDIA: How has gaming evolved over the years that you have been a gamer.

WESTBALLZ: When I started out people thought gaming was something you wasted time on but it's evolved into a fun and competitive career.

CLAUDIA: What perception would you most like to change about how people see gamers?

WESTBALLZ: What I'd like people to understand is that certain games can be as physically demanding as real world sports. You have to be in incredible shape to play them at a pro level.

CLAUDIA: At what point did you first start considering a career in pro video gaming?

WESTBALLZ: When I was in high school. I could really relate to seeing people spend so much time to get good at something they loved.

CLAUDIA: How did your parents react when you told them you wanted to be a pro gamer?

WESTBALLZ: My parents thought it was the biggest waste of time and would always tell me how much more important school was. They've since changed their minds.

> "CERTAIN GAMES CAN BE AS PHYSICALLY DEMANDING AS REAL WORLD SPORTS. YOU HAVE TO BE IN INCREDIBLE SHAPE TO PLAY THEM AT A PRO LEVEL."

CLAUDIA: How did you first enter the pro circuit?

WESTBALLZ: I first started going to house tournaments (where people would host an event at their house) and we would have 20-40 people attend. Then I found out about bigger tournaments and kept attending and getting better until I hit the top ranks.

CLAUDIA: What was your favorite tournament (and why), and what was your least favorite or difficult?

WESTBALLZ: House tournaments because it was a lot more personal and you learned a lot more. The bigger tournaments were a bit more scary 'cause you had to play on a stage where they live streamed it to the internet so there was a lot of pressure to perform well.

CLAUDIA: Do you have a favorite type of controller?

WESTBALLZ: The Gamecube controller because it has the best button layout. You just have more options when it comes to certain button combinations.

CLAUDIA: Do you have a signature move when gaming?

WESTBALLZ: I popularized a certain technique in the game that's widely used by tons of top players. It's a quick two hit attack used when trying to defend the other guy's attacks.

CLAUDIA: What advice would you like to give younger gamers?

WESTBALLZ: Have a balance when it comes to how much time you spend gaming. Make sure you don't overdo it.

CLAUDIA: What feedback would you like to give game developers?

WESTBALLZ: Game developers should understand what makes a game fun. A lot of developers think making the game easier will mean a lot more people will buy and enjoy it but that's not normally the case. People like a challenge and playing games that are too easy doesn't feel rewarding.

WESTBALLZ MEATBALLS

WESTBALLZ MEATBALLS

Everyone loves meatballs, but they can be time consuming when made by hand. This recipe gives you fresh, tasty meatballs in minutes! I've named them after my cousin Weston Dennis a.k.a Westballz. Once you've got these fuelling you, you just might develop reflexes as quick as Weston who's regarded as one of the world's fastest players!

0:02 PREP TIME

0:12 COOK TIME

1 SERVINGS

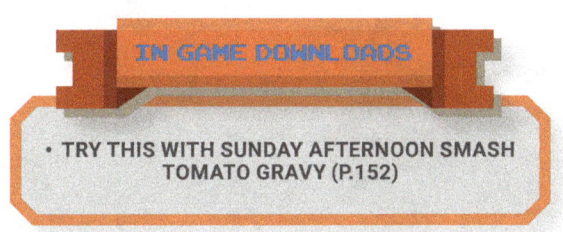

- TRY THIS WITH SUNDAY AFTERNOON SMASH TOMATO GRAVY (P.152)

INGREDIENTS

1 lb ground beef, turkey or chicken
⅓ cup grated Parmesan cheese
1 egg
2 Tbsp breadcrumbs
1 Tbsp Italian seasoning
Pinch of salt, pepper and chili flakes, to taste (optional, the cheese makes the meatballs salty but I always season everything)

METHOD

1. Pre heat oven to 425°.
2. Bind all ingredients together, do NOT over mix.
3. Form golf ball sizes meatballs and place on baking tray-cookie sheet.
4. Bake for about 12 minutes.
5. Coat with marinara sauce and more parmesan if desired and serve.

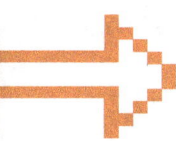

CC'S CRAZY GOAT LAMB SHANKS WITH POLENTA

You're a crazy goat wreaking havoc across the city! Buildings, people and even cars are in your sights as you run rampant! But now you're tired and hungry as a goat! Try some of these lamb shanks and polenta. You and three of your gamer friends can enjoy this one.

Inspired by the video game Goat Simulator

0:15 PREP TIME

4:00 COOK TIME

4 SERVINGS

INGREDIENTS

FOR LAMB:
4 lamb shanks
6 Tbsp olive oil
1 large onion, chopped*
3 large carrots, chopped*
4 celery stalks, chopped*
4 large garlic cloves, minced
1 can (28 oz) diced tomatoes in juice
½–1 whole bottle of red wine (a hearty red is best. If you do not want to use wine then increase the stock ratio and add a few cups of water to cover shanks)

METHOD

1. **Preheat oven to 300-325°F. Season lamb well with salt and pepper.**

2. **Heat 2-3 tablespoons oil in large ovenproof pot over high heat. Add lamb; brown on all sides, about 10 minutes total. Using tongs, transfer lamb to plate.**

3. **Add more oil to pot (a few tablespoons). Add onion, carrots, celery, and garlic. Sauté until vegetables brown and begin to soften, scraping up browned bits, about 10 minutes, don't let garlic burn.**

4. **If using wine add to pot and boil and reduce wine for about 2-4 minutes until alcohol is burned off and wine is slightly reduced.**

5. **Return lamb to pot, add tomatoes, broth, rosemary sprigs, thyme sprigs and bay leaf. Make sure there is enough liquid to barely cover the shanks. Bring to boil over high heat then turn off heat.**

2 cups beef or chicken broth (homemade is best but you can use store bought or even bouillon cubes)

3 large fresh rosemary sprigs

3 large fresh thyme sprigs

1–2 bay leaves

2–6 cups water, depending on whether you are using wine

Italian parsley, chopped, for garnish

FOR POLENTA:

8 cups water

2 tsp salt

2 cups polenta or yellow cornmeal

½ cup (½ stick) butter

1 cup Parmesan cheese, grated

1 Tbsp minced thyme and/or parsley

*if you want to be fancier you can dice everything the same size, but a rough chop still tastes great!

6. Cover pot; transfer to oven leaving a corner of the lid askew so the steam will be released while cooking. Cook until meat is tender and pulls easily from bone, flipping the shanks over once or twice during cooking, about 3-4 hours.

7. Meanwhile, bring 8 cups water and salt to boil in large saucepan over high heat. Gradually whisk in polenta.

8. Reduce heat to medium-low; simmer until thickened and tender, stirring frequently, about 22 minutes.

9. Whisk in butter and minced thyme and/or parsley. Season with salt and pepper and add parmesan and stir (at this point you might wish to switch to a wooden spoon if the mixture is getting stuck in the whisk).

10. Remove lamb and herbs from pot; discard herbs. Place pot over medium-high heat and boil until sauce is slightly thickened, about 5 minutes, taste and season to your taste again with salt and pepper.

11. Divide polenta among 4 large bowls; top each with 1 lamb shank. Pour sauce over; sprinkle a little chopped Italian parsley over it and serve.

SLINGSHOT PORK BRINE

Inspired by the video game Angry Birds

Those cute but feisty angry birds are at it again. They're on a mission to topple the myriad of elaborate structures that their nemesis – the Hogs – have erected in their path. But these birds aren't bird-brains. They have a giant slingshot and aren't afraid to hurl themselves into the fray to topple the pork empire! While you help these birds wreak havok on the legion of swine, you may develop a taste for some pork, yourself. You've got some pork chops in the freezer or a chicken and you're not sure of the date or the quality but hey, you don't want to waste food, right? It's an insult to the animal and to the environment. So what to do? Brine it! This will enable you to seal in some great flavor before you cook it. It may be the breakthrough you need to reach the next level of Angry Birds!

PREP TIME 12:00
COOK TIME 0:35
SERVINGS 3-4

INGREDIENTS

3–4 frozen pork chops (frozen chicken pieces also work well)

FOR BRINE:
6–8 cups water (enough to cover the meat)
½ cup brown or white sugar
½ cup salt
2–3 bay leaves
2 Tbsp allspice berries (or fennel seeds)
2 Tbsp peppercorns
1 onion, quartered
3 garlic cloves, smashed

METHOD

TO BRINE THE MEAT:

1. In the morning before you stumble off to work, put all ingredients for brine into a large soup or stock pot (an 8-quart pot is best). Place pork chops into brine and put lid on. If it's a larger piece of meat, then increase the ration of salt and sugar as well as water.

2. Let sit for up to 12 hours. Pork will thaw and be well-brined. If you live in a very hot area and don't use air conditioning then stick the whole pot in the fridge if you're going to be gone a long time and fear that it will thaw out and get warm, use common sense folks. I leave mine out on the counter with or without a lid, yes, I'm a renegade.

FOR COOKING:
2 tsp oil
1 garlic clove, minced
¼ cup chicken stock (or wine)
1 onion, sliced (optional)
2 Tbsp fennel seeds (optional)
Pinch of pepper flakes

TO COOK:

3. Pre-heat oven to 400°. Remove pork chops from brine and pat dry. Place a couple teaspoons of oil in a pan and pan fry chops for 2 minutes per side, until chops are browned.

4. Remove chops from pan and place into a baking dish. Sautee some sliced onions and/or fennel and add a pinch of pepper flakes and cook for about a minute, then put in baking dish with pork.

5. Add the chicken stock or wine and bake for 20-25 minutes. Then allow pork to rest for 5 minutes before serving. This dish goes well with mashed potatoes, vegetables, applesauce or whatever you like to serve with it.

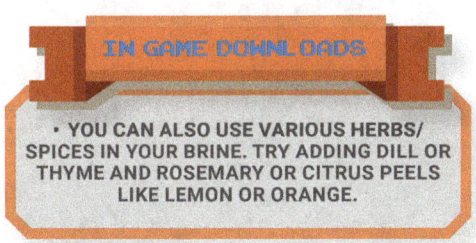

IN GAME DOWNLOADS
- YOU CAN ALSO USE VARIOUS HERBS/SPICES IN YOUR BRINE. TRY ADDING DILL OR THYME AND ROSEMARY OR CITRUS PEELS LIKE LEMON OR ORANGE.

HACK ATTACK!

QUICK BUTTERMILK

If you don't have buttermilk on hand, but want to try making some, here's a simple recipe to make your own – and earn triple bonus gamer points!

Pour 1 cup of milk into a bowl. Add a tablespoon or two of fresh lemon juice or white vinegar and stir to combine. Let sit a minute until you see it curdle.

Use in place of buttermilk in the recipe as it calls for. Enjoy!

QUICK METRO CHICKEN KIEV

The year is 2033 and Mother Russia is slowly coming back to life after World War III. The radiation is starting to fade, but the surface isn't very safe for humans yet. Mutated wild animals abound, and you have to deal with the Dark Ones - who have psychic abilities that cause hallucinations to anyone who comes into proximity of them. You need to reach Exhibition and re-activate the lone military silo, in order to put an end to the Dark Ones once and for all. You have a long way to go so grab a mutant chicken and try out this quick recipe!

0:10 PREP TIME

0:50 COOK TIME

2-4 SERVINGS

INGREDIENTS

- ⅔ cup butter
- ½ cup Italian-style breadcrumbs
- 2 Tbsp Parmesan cheese
- 1 Tbsp Italian seasoning
- 1 tsp garlic salt
- 4 boneless chicken breast halves
- ¼ cup green onion, chopped
- ¼ cup parsley, chopped
- ¼ cup white wine

METHOD

1. Pre-heat oven to 375°. Melt butter.

2. Combine breadcrumbs, cheese, Italian seasoning and garlic salt.

3. Dip chicken in melted butter, then coat with breadcrumb mixture. Reserve remaining melted butter for later.

4. Place chicken into an ungreased pan and bake for 45 minutes.

5. While chicken is baking, combine wine, green onions and parsley to the remaining butter.

6. Pour new mixture over chicken and continue baking 5 more minutes, then serve.

Inspired by the video game Metro 2033

"I WAS HAPPY TO BE WORKING WITH YOU CLAUDIA, SINCE WE'VE KNOWN EACH OTHER FOR SO LONG. I ALSO REMEMBER THAT SMALL ASS COCKPIT."

VOICE ACTOR PROFILE
GARY HUDSON

GARY has had a long career as an actor and has been in films such as Roadhouse alongside Patrick Swayze, TV shows Dallas and Suits and most recently the movie Fifty Shades Freed. He also has one video game appearance on his resume, a game that I also appeared in—Solar Eclipse for the Sega Saturn. It was one of the early games in 1995 that utilized full motion video within the actual game. He played the character of Lt. Jake Cross (call sign Stuntman), while I portrayed Major Delany Kelt (call sign Raven). It was the one voice gig where they actually put me in a mockup of a fighter ship's cockpit!

CLAUDIA: I'm sure our readers would like to know, do you enjoy cooking and if so, what's your best dish?

GARY: Being from the south I'm a great griller and breakfast cook thanks to my Uncle Joe who would make us breakfast after church on Sunday. He taught me to make grits, fried apples, great hash browns with peppers and onions and banana pancakes. I love making salads and cooking salmon and the occasional New York steak and, in the holidays, my mom's broccoli casserole — a hit at Christmas and Thanksgiving.

CLAUDIA: Back in 1995 you and I were in the game Solar Eclipse — a space shooter game that had us performing our parts in a movie-like video, what do you remember about that?

GARY: I remember we had a great time doing it and I was happy to be working with you Claudia, since we've known each other for so long. I also remember that small ass cockpit. It was a lot of fun and there was a short production schedule so the days were long.

CLAUDIA: Have you ever played a video game, and if so, what is your favorite?

GARY: I'm not a gamer but have played some with my nephews back in Virginia. Really enjoyed "Call of Duty". Afraid if I started playing in LA, I wouldn't be able to stop.

SPACE SHOOTER ROASTED CHICKEN

In 1995, Solar Eclipse was released for the Sega Saturn game system. I don't recall much from Solar Eclipse since it was my first game ever. I do remember being stuck into a fake cockpit and having a cheat sheet of my lines taped to one of the consoles. Co-star Gary Hudson and I became fast friends and the whole thing was new and interesting to me. Little did I know that I would spend the next 20+ years doing games! While you're out trying to save Titan from marauding aliens and trying your best to not get sunburn, try making this tasty chicken recipe. This recipe will serve 2-6 gamers depending on how hungry they are and if you have multiple side dishes. When your gaming friends comment how awesome your cooking is, you can confidently reply, "We don't do circus tricks around here!"

0:08 PREP TIME

1:00 COOK TIME

2-6 SERVINGS

INGREDIENTS

1 whole chicken rinsed and dried, innards removed
Salt and pepper
1 lemon cut in half
2-3 garlic cloves, smashed
Olive oil
Herbs (optional)

METHOD

1. Pre heat oven to 425°. Generously salt the cavity of the chicken. Put the halves of lemon and the garlic and herbs, if using, in the cavity of the chicken.

2. Rub the whole chicken with olive oil then salt and pepper it. Place on a lined baking sheet and cook at 400° for one hour. The high heat is imperative for this recipe and it's why it only takes an hour and ends up juicy and delicious.

3. Pierce the thigh to make sure the juices run clear. Remove from oven and let rest for 5 minutes. Carve and enjoy!

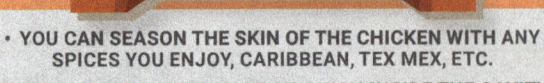

- YOU CAN SEASON THE SKIN OF THE CHICKEN WITH ANY SPICES YOU ENJOY, CARIBBEAN, TEX MEX, ETC.
- YOU CAN ALSO PUT A HALF AN ONION INSIDE THE CAVITY, FRESH ROSEMARY, DILL, PARSLEY... ANYTHING REALLY.

Inspired by the video game Solar Eclipse

HACK ATTACK!

WASTE NOT ROASTED CHICKEN

I have respect for the chicken and think it's a waste to carve off some meat then throw the carcass in the bin. Whether it's a chicken you roast yourself or one ready to go from your local supermarket, there are a few things you can do if you have a little time and some leftover veggies.

Soup! Everyone loves chicken soup and it's great to have in the freezer in case you have nothing for dinner or it's chilly and you feel a cold coming on. After enjoying the meat from the chicken, pick off all of the little pieces you missed and set aside. Check the back of the chicken for the tender morsels there. You can use the leftover chicken meat for salads. Just add mayo and mustard and some chopped celery, salt and pepper.

Remove as much skin as you can from the carcass and discard the skin, break the carcass into a few pieces. Put the carcass in a big pot, cover with water by a few inches and add whatever veggies you have in the fridge: carrot, celery, onion, fennel, etc... You can put some parsley and a bay leaf in if you have some.

Don't bother chopping them nicely, this is just for the stock. An Italian chef taught me that you don't even have to peel the onion or the veggies, just chop them roughly and toss them in. Then cook the heck out of the whole lot. Bring to a boil, reduce to a simmer then cook for 3-6 hours.

Stir it once in a while. If the water reduces too much add a little more. After a few hours of simmering turn it off and let it cool.

To remove the fat on the surface, I just gently put a paper towel on top of the cooled stock and let it absorb the oil then repeat until there is no oil on the paper towel (discard paper towel).

Strain the stock in a colander; discard the bones, veggies, and herbs.

Put the stock back into a large pot and add your favorite soup veggies, chopped to your liking (rough or fine). Celery, onion and carrot is classic but I like zucchini and fennel and cabbage too. Bring to a simmer and reduce. You can add some pasta or grains and I always add a tablespoon or more of good quality chicken bouillon, even a single cube will give it more depth and saltiness.

Season to taste and when veggies and pasta are done you have a nutritious, fast soup to enjoy. Serve with a salad and crusty bread!

IN GAME DOWNLOADS

- IF YOU DON'T HAVE BUTTERMILK, SEE THE HACK ON P.69 FOR HOW TO MAKE SOME!

BREAKAWAY HOCKEY CHICKEN PARMESAN

In the middle of a fast-paced game of NHL 2018 and need a something to eat before the 3rd Period begins? Try making some of this amazing chicken parmesan that is so quick, you'll think you're on a 2-on-1 breakaway, heading to the net! It's easy to make and can be doubled pretty easily, depending on the number of teammates you need to feed. This recipe will be ready in a jiff, and you'll soon be blasting past the defenders on your way to a hat-trick and the Stanley Cup.

Inspired by the video game NHL 2018

6:00 PREP TIME

0:30 COOK TIME

1-2 SERVINGS

INGREDIENTS

- 1-2 boneless, skinless chicken breasts, sliced into fingers
- 2 cups bread crumbs
- 3 cups water
- 1 cup buttermilk
- ½ cup marinara sauce
- ½ cup shredded mozzarella cheese (or your favorite cheese slices)
- 1 package Ramen noodles

METHOD

1. Pour buttermilk into a plastic container and season with your favorite seasonings or hot sauce. Place chicken breasts into mixture and store covered in the refrigerator for 4 hours.

2. Remove chicken from buttermilk mixture and coat with breadcrumbs. Store on a baking sheet in the oven for at least 2 hours to allow breadcrumbs to adhere to chicken well.

3. Preheat oven to 425°. Spread chicken fingers onto a foil-lined baking sheet. Cook chicken 15 minutes, then flip and cook another 15 minutes. With 2 minutes left on cooking time, put some shredded cheese (or sliced cheese) on top of chicken to melt.

4. Meanwhile, microwave 3 cups water in microwave for 3 minutes, place Ramen Noodles in heated water and set aside to get noodles tender. When noodles are al dente, place in strainer to drain water.

5. Heat up 1 cup of your favorite tomato sauce and pour over top of the chicken and noodles for a delicious chicken parmesan.

BILLY EGG'S SPICY-TANGY CHICKEN THIGHS

You and your friends have been playing Super Alfred Chicken all afternoon, trying to rescue Bill Egg and his brothers from their captors with Alfred's amazing bionic beak (watch out for the deadly meka-chickens). Now you are all hungry for what else – chicken! This recipe makes enough for you and 3 of your gaming buddies.

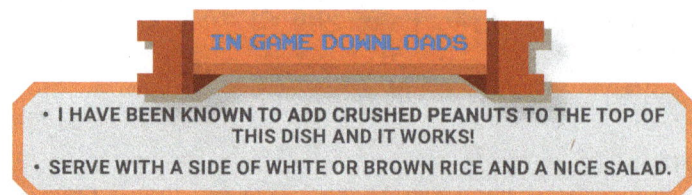

IN GAME DOWNLOADS
- I HAVE BEEN KNOWN TO ADD CRUSHED PEANUTS TO THE TOP OF THIS DISH AND IT WORKS!
- SERVE WITH A SIDE OF WHITE OR BROWN RICE AND A NICE SALAD.

INGREDIENTS

4 cloves garlic, peeled
1 small onion, quartered
1 Tbsp fresh oregano, or 1 tsp dried
2 tsp ground cumin
¼ tsp cayenne, or to taste
Salt and pepper
1 Tbsp oil
2 Tbsp each of orange juice AND freshly squeezed lime juice
About 1½ lb boneless chicken thighs, or 2 lb thighs with bones, with or without skin
Chopped cilantro, for serving

METHOD

1. Preheat your grill or broiler to medium-high. Combine the garlic, onion, oregano, cumin, cayenne, cloves, salt, pepper and oil in a blender or small food processor, and blend until fairly smooth.

2. Add the juices, season to taste. It should pack a punch.

3. Pour sauce over chicken and let marinate for about 30 minutes.

4. Grill 6 to 8 minutes a side, or until meat is nicely browned and cooked medium or better on the inside. (Thighs with bones will take longer, about 20 minutes total.)

5. Serve with cilantro sprinkled on top and lime wedges.

Inspired by the video game Super Alfred Chicken

RAPTURE DEEP SEA SALMON

You have taken the mysterious bathysphere down to an oceanic utopia called Rapture, in the game Bioshock, and you enter a world created by the greatest thinkers of the time, but what you realize along the way is that the scientific discovery of the genetic material called ADAM – which enhances a person's mental abilities with various affects – has driven the inhabitants of Rapture crazy. If only they had stuck to eating wonderfully cooked salmon, like the following recipe, instead of experimenting on themselves, perhaps Rapture would have less chaos, and more harmony, and there wouldn't be a need for the Big Daddys that strike fear in those who provoke them!

0:05 PREP TIME

0:15 COOK TIME

1-2 SERVINGS

INGREDIENTS

1–2 salmon filets
2 tsp olive oil
1 tsp fresh herbs
Salt and pepper, to taste
Sliced limes or lemons (optional)

Inspired by the video game Bioshock

METHOD

1. Preheat the oven to 425°. Rub the salmon filet with olive oil and season with salt and pepper

2. Chop up some fresh herbs like dill or chives or parsley (I use small scissors to cut my chives it's much easier). You can put some sliced lemons or limes or even oranges on top.

3. Put salmon in an oven proof pan or dish and stick in the preheated oven then turn the oven off and walk away and forget about it for about 15 minutes. Remove from oven, the salmon will be perfectly cooked and not dry.

IN GAME DOWNLOADS

- INSTEAD OF USING PLAIN OLIVE OIL, SEE MY FISH HACKS FOR SPICING UP THE RUB. AND, IF YOU HAVE TIME, YOU CAN INCREASE THE FLAVOR BY MARINATING THE SALMON (P.152).
- TRY ADDING A SAUCE AFTERWARDS (SEE P.152 FOR A QUICK AND DELICIOUS RECIPE).

MARK'S LIFE HACKS

HAVING cerebral palsy, I've been using crutches for the better part of my life and so I've come up with some crazy hacks so I could join in activities with my non-handicapped friends—taping a hockey blade to my wooden crutches when I was nine so I could play street hockey in Philadelphia (much to my mom's horror) or installing mini-headlights into the handles of my aluminum crutches as a teen. I must have picked up the habit from my grandfather on my dad's side who invented a hack to help me walk.

Up until I was six years old, when I wanted to get around, I would either crawl, use a custom-built belly board that my paternal grandfather built for me out of some casters and a nice piece of wood, or my mother would carry me over her shoulder like a sack of potatoes. When I took my first steps in full-leg braces and forearm crutches, I needed to learn how to walk. The therapists put me into a pair of low-level parallel bars and my legs, due to their scissoring, were separated by an upright piece of 2x4 as I walked. Not easy!

My grandfather took it upon himself to replicate the parallel bars from my therapist's office at home, using copper pipes. He made the bars to my specific height, then added a longer piece of wood to further separate my legs, and help me actually learn how to walk using the four-point gait—the method most people on crutches would use to ambulate. While I hated using it for forty-five minutes each day to supplement the therapy sessions, Grandpa's bars helped me learn to walk much more quickly. Nowadays, with the increasing pain of torn shoulder muscles, I have to use a power wheelchair, but the hacks continue, especially food hacks so I can continue cooking.

> "I HAVE TO USE A POWER WHEELCHAIR, BUT THE HACKS CONTINUE, ESPECIALLY FOOD HACKS SO I CAN CONTINUE COOKING."

HACK #1: Wrap my toaster oven's cookie sheet with foil and bake off bratwurst or hot dogs, instead of boiling them.

HACK #2: Substitute Ramen noodles in lieu of spaghetti noodles! You can obtain the same consistency with Ramen noodles that you get from perfectly boiled pasta, simply by allowing the ramen noodles to steep in pre-boiled water from the microwave (See Surviving Cryostasis Spaghetti, p.60).

HACK #3: Light-weight plates, pans or even paper plates have helped reduce the strain on my shoulders, come clean up time!

ANTI-DRACULA GARLIC CHICKEN

Don't venture into Castlevania and take on Dracula and his army without the added power of garlic breath to ward off any undead you encounter along the way. If Dracula isn't overcome by your garlic breath you can try offering him leftovers of this delicious dish and then driving a stake through his heart while he's distracted. This recipe feeds one or two famished vampire hunters.

0:08 PREP TIME

0:30 COOK TIME

1-2 SERVINGS

INGREDIENTS

- 1–2 boneless, skinless chicken breasts*
- ½ medium onion, sliced thick
- 1–2 Tbsp minced garlic
- 4 pats butter
- ½ cup chicken stock
- ½ tsp Italian seasoning

METHOD

1. Preheat oven to 350°. Place onions in bottom of oven-safe dish, then pour chicken stock over them.

2. Place unwrapped chicken breasts over the onions. Sprinkle chicken with seasonings.

3. Top with even amount of garlic and place pat of butter on each piece of chicken. Bake for 27 to 30 minutes. Serve with your favorite side dish.

*If chicken breasts are frozen, no need to thaw, simply bake approximately 10 extra minutes until juices run clear in chicken.

Inspired by the game Castlevania for the Nintendo Entertainment System

IN GAME DOWNLOADS

- IF SERVING WITH RICE OR COUSCOUS, CONSIDER ADDING SOME RAISINS AND ALMOND SLIVERS TO THE GRAIN OF YOUR CHOICE.
- IF YOU LIKE FRESH CILANTRO, IT GOES VERY WELL IN AND/OR ON THIS CHICKEN DISH.
- YOU CAN ADD SOME FRESH GRATED GINGER TO THE DISH WHEN YOU ARE COOKING THE SHALLOT (OR ONION).
- YOU CAN ADD A MINCED HOT PEPPER OF YOUR LIKING AT THE SAME TIME AS THE SHALLOT OR ONION FOR HEAT.
- YOU CAN ADD FRESH MINCED GARLIC WHEN SAUTÉING THE SHALLOT OR ONION.

FREEWAY CHICKEN MADRAS

In the game Freeway, chickens are in an awful hurry to cross the freeway, but no one knows why. Maybe they're just showing off their adventurous side, like you can by making this super-fast and easy, curry-inspired chicken dish you can serve with rice or couscous. You and four of your friends will be racing each other to gobble this up!

Inspired by the 1981 video game Freeway

0:10 PREP TIME

0:11 COOK TIME

4-5 SERVINGS

INGREDIENTS

- 4 boneless, skinless chicken breasts, cut into 2–3-inch pieces
- 2 Tbsp olive oil
- Salt and pepper, to taste
- 1 large zucchini, cut into rounds (ends cut off and discarded)
- 2 tsp curry powder
- 1 Tbsp butter
- 2 Tbsp shallots, finely chopped (you can use onion or scallion if you don't have shallots)
- ½ cup chicken broth
- 2 Tbsp heavy cream

METHOD

1. Put chicken pieces in a bowl big enough to hold and the zucchini and add 1 tablespoon of the oil, and salt and pepper. Add zucchini and curry powder to the chicken and blend well with clean hands to coat the pieces evenly.

2. Heat the remaining tablespoon of oil in a sturdy pan/skillet and add the chicken pieces in one layer. Scatter the zucchini rounds between the chicken pieces in one layer. Cook over medium-high heat until chicken pieces are nicely browned on one side, about 3 minutes. Turn the chicken pieces and the zucchini rounds and cook over medium-low heat about 5 minutes. Transfer to a warm serving dish.

3. Pour off the fat from the skillet and add the butter. Add shallots and cook, stirring, about 30 seconds. Add broth and cook until reduced to about cup. Add cream, stir and bring to a boil. Return chicken and zucchini pieces to the sauce and turn the pieces in the sauce. Cook about 2 minutes then serve hot.

VOICE ACTOR PROFILE

ROBIN ATKIN DOWNES

ROBIN Atkin Downes has appeared in the films How to Train Your Dragon, Steamboy and Superman vs. The Elite, TV shows including Angel, Avengers: Earth's Mightiest Heroes, Buffy the Vampire Slayer, Star Wars: The Clone Wars and ThunderCats as well as video games such as Gears of War, Metal Gear, No More Heroes, Kingdom Hearts, Ratchet & Clank, Saints Row: The Third, as the Medic in Team Fortress 2, The Elder Scrolls V: Skyrim, The Last of Us, Tomb Raider, Uncharted and X-Men Legends. I first had the opportunity to work with him on the feature-length Babylon 5 episode In the Beginning. He also played the part of Byron in the same show.

CLAUDIA: What's your favourite dish?

ROBIN: Burnt Hand Chicken. It's cooked with herbes de provence, chicken stock and white wine. The preparation requires sautéing the chicken then baking it for 20 minutes and then finishing on the stove top, which is where the name comes from. I usually forget how hot the pan is, especially when I'm drinking wine while cooking, which I usually do!

CLAUDIA: You've voiced so many video game characters, I have to ask; have you ever played any of the games you voiced?

ROBIN: Yes, I've played many of them. It's research and a great write off!

CLAUDIA: Having been in so many video games, is there one you consider to be your favorite? And why?

ROBIN: That's a tough question... There are so many great games! I think the Uncharted franchise... Because I worked on the game for so many years with so many great characters. Navarro, Tenzin, Talbot and Alcazar. It's also a fantastic game to play. The train scene in Uncharted 2 is epic!

CLAUDIA: I see that you have been in Assassin's Creed 3, where you voiced General George Washington. How did you approach voicing such an historical character – what was your motivation?

ROBIN: Interesting that you ask about that character as he's connected to a lot of great food. After recording for the main game I was asked to fly up to Montreal to shoot performance capture for The Tyranny of George Washington. I spent three separate weeks from September to November, watching the season change from fall to winter, and ate at many of the restaurants in town whenever I had the chance. I tasted some of the most amazing dishes I've ever had in my life. Usually the motivation for a character comes from the page. In great games like Assassin's Creed the characters are clearly-defined and you just fall into them.

CLAUDIA: Have you ever been to Valley Forge Park, the locale for Assassins Creed 3?

ROBIN: Yes! One of my favorite memories was driving from Los Angeles to Philadelphia where I attended graduate school for theatre. I remember stopping outside the city at Valley Forge. It's such a huge part of American history, and a testament to the human potential.

CLAUDIA: Can you recall the first video game you auditioned for? Did you get that gig?

ROBIN: I think one of the first big ones was Halo 2 for the Prophet of Regret. A very ambitious and fun villain to play. And... What an asshole! Another great game that I enjoyed playing at the time.

CLAUDIA: Have you found more fandom from your voice career or from your on-camera career?

ROBIN: It's nice to see a new generation of Babylon 5 fans out there, but there is so much memorabilia for the games and cartoons, so I'd say more from my voice career.

CLAUDIA: For you, which is more difficult, voice acting or traditional acting?

ROBIN: I enjoy the challenges of all mediums. I've been fortunate to explore, Theatre, Film, TV, Performance capture and Voice Acting. I hope to continue being challenged and creatively fulfilled by working, playing games and cooking! And... Drinking great wine!

> "*In great games like Assassin's Creed the characters are clearly-defined and you just fall into them.*"

ROBIN ATKIN DOWNES AT THE 2013 PHOENIX COMICON IN PHOENIX, ARIZONA.

DRAGON BORN BURNT HAND CHICKEN

My fellow Babylon 5 actor and friend Robin Atkin Downes appears as the thief Brynjolf in The Elder Scrolls V: Skyrim. He graciously provided us with us his recipe for Burnt Hand Chicken, so adventurous gamers could try making it themselves. The name derives from the fact that you have to pop the whole pan into the oven to finish the cooking, and if you're drinking wine whilst cooking, you might just forget how hot the pan is and burn your hand. So, let that be a warning!

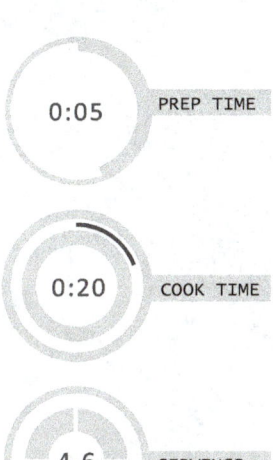

0:05 PREP TIME

0:20 COOK TIME

4-6 SERVINGS

Inspired by the video game The Elder Scrolls V: Skyrim

INGREDIENTS

1 chicken (3 lb)
2 Tbsp butter
¼ cup Herbs de Provence
1 cup chicken stock
½ cup white wine
2 cloves garlic, finely chopped
1 tsp salt
½ tsp pepper

METHOD

1. Pre-heat oven to 375°. Put the Herbs de Provence on the chicken with the salt and pepper and brown both sides in a pan with a little butter.

2. Add some wine, chicken stock, and garlic and fill the pan so the top of the chicken where the skin is is still visible.

3. Let the sauce reduce a little bit then throw it in the oven at 375° for 15 to 20 minutes.

4. Take it out the oven and back to the stove top to reduce the sauce more, being careful not to burn your hands when removing the pan from the oven!

IN GAME DOWNLOADS

- ROBIN SOMETIMES TAKE THE CHICKEN OUT AT THE LAST MINUTE AND QUICKLY BROILS IT TO GET THE SKIN VERY CRISPY BEFORE SERVING WITH THE SAUCE... HE USUALLY SERVES IT WITH FRESH SAUTÉED SPINACH AND ROASTED FINGERLING POTATOES.
- FOR ADDED ASSASSIN'S CREED POINTS, YOU CAN MAKE YOUR OWN HERBS DE PROVENCE (P.91).

HACK ATTACK!

HERBS AND FANCY FRENCH HERBS

Fresh herbs can turn a good meal into a great one - here are some hacks to make using fresh herbs easy! You can even make your own fancy French herbs!

HACK #1: Here's a hack that will make removing stems from herbs simple! First get a clean colander and place the stem of the herb in one of the holes in the colander, pull through from the opposite side and voila! The herb leaves stay in the colander while the stems are in your hand. You can save the stems in a baggie in the freezer to add to the stock pot or just throw them away.

HACK #2: If a recipe calls for a deeper flavor of herbs use a mortar and pestle to grind them with a bit of salt to release the oils and make a paste. This is a good method for herbs in minestrone or for a pesto, etc.

HACK #3: When chopping fine herbs like chives, dill or tarragon, try using clean, sharp scissors to snip them into small pieces instead of chopping them with a knife on a cutting board. Not only will you retain the precious and delicious oils from the herbs but you will also have a much easier clean up.

HACK #4: If chopping herbs and garlic or shallots for a recipe try chopping them together, e.g., parsley and shallots or basil and garlic. The herbs will keep the garlic or shallots from rolling around the cutting board and you will end up with a nice uniformly chopped mixture.

HERBS DE PROVENCE

INGREDIENTS:

2 Tbsp dried rosemary
2 Tbsp deied savory
2 Tbsp dried thyme
2 Tbsp dried marjoram
1 Tbsp dried parsley

METHOD:

Put all ingredients into a spice blender and grind well. Empty grinder into a shaker jar, store in pantry for later use. Makes enough for a 9 oz shaker of spice mix.

"Not only will you retain the precious and delicious oils from the herbs but you will also have a much easier clean up."

SPORT FISH HALIBUT WITH CABBAGE & POTATOES

Fishing on the high seas has never been more fun than on the Dreamcast. Simply toss your line into the ocean and start reeling. If you're lucky you may get a grouper, stingray, shark or even a large halibut! You're going to work up an appetite, so why not make a great meal with actual halibut and throw in some hearty veggies and potatoes? This recipe can be made beforehand, so you can enjoy a relaxing evening fishing. It may look as intimidating as pulling in a 400lb shark, but hold your nerve and you'll find it isn't too difficult after all.

Inspired by the video game Marine Fishing

1:00 PREP TIME

0:15 COOK TIME

8 SERVINGS

INGREDIENTS

8 halibut filets

8–12 baby potatoes, halved

⅛ cup (or more) olive oil

1 whole Savoy cabbage or small head of red or green cabbage, quartered

1 tsp salt

½ tsp pepper

2 tsp Herbs de Provence, fresh or dried herbs like parsley, thyme, basil, tarragon

Lemon or lime juice, to taste

Zingy layer - something to give the dish a bit of a zing! Try a handful of capers, or chopped scallions with fresh chopped parsley.

METHOD

1. Pre heat oven to 425°. Put baby potatoes in a pan, toss with oil and season.
2. Rub the cabbage with oil and season with salt and pepper, place in pan with potatoes, sprinkle with herbs de Provence or whatever herb blend you like.
3. Roast for 15-25 minutes until veggies are tender and browning a bit (you want them beginning to caramelize before you add the fish).
4. In the meantime, rub halibut with oil. Remove pan and add halibut. Season with salt and pepper and/or any spice blend you like and maybe a squirt or lemon or lime juice or zest and another little glug of olive oil.
5. Place back in oven for 10-15 minutes depending on the thickness of your fish (it should be opaque but don't over cook it, see if it flakes easily and remember it cooks a little more when you take it out of the oven).
6. Remove pan and add something zingy like a handful of capers, chopped scallions with fresh chopped parsley and another squirt of lemon and serve!

THE FURIOUS FIVE'S SALMON FOIL MEAL

In the game Kung Fu Panda – you take on the role of Po, the large panda who metes out justice with some funny humor. Master Po Ping and the other Kung-Fu masters are always training in case they are called upon to defend the people once more. Training all day takes a lot of energy and strength, so they need something tasty to replenish their energy, but not weigh them down. They make a delectable dish that comes in a handy foil pouch; The Furious Five Salmon Foil Meal! Prepped and cooked inside a foil pack, this dish does not take long to cook and tastes yummy enough to satisfy even Master Po Ping's legendary appetite!

Inspired by the video game Kung-Fu Panda

0:05 PREP TIME

0:10 COOK TIME

1-2 SERVINGS

INGREDIENTS

- 2 salmon filets or one large filet weighing about 1 lb (if it's frozen, defrost first and rinse with water and dry well)
- 1 lime, thinly sliced
- ½ cup scallions, sliced
- 1 jalapeño pepper, thinly sliced
- 1–2 Tbsp of soy sauce
- 1 Tbsp sesame or olive oil (for an Asian flavor use sesame, or to highlight the jalapeño flavor, use olive oil)
- Pinch of salt
- 1 tsp brown sugar
- 2 Tbsp water
- Cilantro leaves (optional)

METHOD

1. Preheat oven to 400°. Take a large piece of tin foil and place sliced limes, scallions and jalapeños in a pile large enough to go under your salmon filet. Sprinkle a few teaspoons of soy sauce over the whole pile.

2. Place your salmon filet over the pile and sprinkle with more soy sauce and sesame oil or olive oil depending on your taste. Season with salt and pepper and a teaspoon of brown sugar sprinkled over the fish then squeeze some lime juice over the whole thing and a few tablespoons of water as well.

3. Tightly seal the tinfoil into a package with the seam on top and the sides crimped tightly shut. Place on a small baking sheet to prevent spills and cook for about 10 minutes depending on the thickness of your salmon (you can pop it out and stick a knife in it to check on it just be careful of the steam that will come out of the hot foil!).

Enjoy with rice, salad or simple steamed or boiled green beans with a quick vinaigrette or your favorite salad dressing or soy sauce and sesame oil or butter... whatever you like!

IN GAME DOWNLOADS

- IF YOU'RE NOT A FAN OF SALMON, TRY USING BONELESS, SKINLESS FLOUNDER OR ANY FISH FOR THAT MATTER, ADJUST THE TIME FOR THINNER FILETS!
- YOU CAN ALSO DO THIS ON THE BBQ, PLACING THE FOIL PACKET DIRECTLY OVER THE HOT GRILL.

"IT WAS REFRESHING TO WORK ON A MOVIE THAT STEPPED OUT OF THE USUAL DISNEY FORMULA."

A LOST CITY IN DEEP BLUE WATERS

I'VE always wanted to be in a Disney animated film, I mean who hasn't? The directors and producer of Disney's first animated science fiction film liked my performance in Babylon 5 and hired me to play Lieutenant Helga Katrina Sinclair the femme fatale-bad ass who went up against James Garner's Commander Lyle Rourke and set Michael J Fox's character, Milo James Thatch, on a mission to the great lost city of Atlantis.

It was refreshing to work on a movie that stepped out of the usual Disney formula. My character was tough, ruthless and the actual princess in the film, Kida, voiced by Cree Summer (who I also worked with in Strange Love, a bizarre animated feature by GB Haim) was no pushover either.

I arrived to work at the Disney studio where they recorded Snow White, feeling just a little intimidated. As I was going in for my recording session, Demi Moore, who had been recording The Hunchback of Notre Dame, was walking out. I had a blast finding Helga's "sexy-Kathleen Turner" voice and then switching gears to her bonkers angry Lieutenant commandeering voice. The team was so fun and supportive, and it was such a joy. It took a few years to finish the project and over that time animators video taped my voice sessions and started to draw Helga. I was shocked when I saw her, she looked like a blond version of me! My eyebrows, my expressions... all of it was captured in this energetic, complex character that I was lucky enough to help bring to life.

But this is a book about gaming, so I should tell you about my work on Atlantis: the Lost Empire and its sequel where I reprised my role as Helga Sinclair.

In the game, the player takes control of Milo and the other characters Vinny, Audrey and Moleire as they traverse Atlantis and rescue Princess Kida, finally saving Atlantis itself from doom. The game version of Atlantis was released for the Playstation console and the Gameboy Advance and Gameboy Color hand-held gaming systems. Initial game-related publications considered the Atlantis game an "uninspired first-person-shooter", but it still performed fairly well in sales; enough to warrant a sequel: Atlantis: The Lost Empire – Trial by Fire. This installment of the game was for PC only and did not get ported to any console.

And now a recipe inspired by the game. How about an Atlantis ceviche? I was thinking of finding a lost city in the deep blue waters when I put it together.

AT THE DISNEY ATLANTIS PREMIERE WITH THE CAST AND CREW, INCLUDING MICHAEL J. FOX

HELGA'S CEVICHE

In the game Atlantis, you take on the role of Milo Thatch, a quirky college cartographer, who believes he knows the location of the lost city of Atlantis but hasn't been able to secure the funds to actually locate it. Making your way through the game, you try to avoid Helga Sinclair, along with her band of mercenaries – who are not just looking for the lost city for historical purposes, but for riches beyond imagination. While you're working out all of the elaborate puzzles in this game, which unlock info that points you to the location of Atlantis, you may need something tasty to keep your brain and reflexes going. Why not make some of this wonderful Ceviche? It's easy to make and won't hamper your gameplay. You can make enough to serve one or more gamers without too much effort.

4:00 PREP TIME

0:02 COOK TIME

2-4 SERVINGS

INGREDIENTS

1 lb shrimp
¼-½ red onion, diced or very thinly sliced*
1 cucumber, diced
1 jalapeño chili or ¼ habanero chili (I prefer the taste and heat level of jalapeño)
3 tomatoes, diced
½ bunch of cilantro, finely chopped
½ cup fresh lime juice
½ cup strained passionfruit juice or orange juice
Juice from one lemon
Salt and pepper, to taste
1 avocado
Tostada or corn chips, to serve

METHOD

1. Blanche shrimp in boiling water for about 1 minute, then shock in ice-cold water. Strain when cooled.

2. Cut shrimp into 1-inch pieces and add to bowl. Add citrus juices and marinate for 2 hours.

3. Add red onion, tomatoes, chilies and cilantro, marinate for 2 more hours.

4. Add avocados and cucumber before serving. Serve in a bowl with chips on the side or on top of tostadas.

* Amount depends on how much onion you like. If you hate raw onion taste like I do, then see the hack on p.37

Inspired by the video game Atlantis: The Lost Empire for the Playstation

IN GAME DOWNLOADS

- ADD IN SOME FRESH PAPAYA, IF YOU ENJOY FRUIT IN YOUR MEAL!
- THIS CAN EITHER BE AN APPETIZER, OR A FULL-ON ENTRÉE. JUST PLAN ON EACH PERSON HAVING 2 TO 3 TOSTADAS FOR AN ENTRÉE.

HACK ATTACK!

FANCY 5-MINUTE SCALLOPS

Most people avoid cooking scallops because they are expensive and if you overcook them they turn rubbery. But with this quick and easy scallop hack, you can make a fancy dinner in just 5 minutes!

The easiest, fastest way to make them is to take the scallops out of the fridge, and dry them off and season them with salt and pepper and let them rest so they come to room temperature.

In a large pan that fits all of the scallops without touching each other, melt a few tablespoons of butter with the same amount of oil and when it's hot and foamy but not brown, add the scallops and cook until they are golden brown—about 2 minutes.

Then flip over and cook the same amount of time. Honestly, even the big ones only take about 4 minutes total to cook.

At the end of cooking, remove the scallops and place on the serving dish. Squirt some fresh lemon juice in the pan and swirl it around with the leftover cooking liquid and butter and oil then pour that over the scallops. Sprinkle with chopped parsley (optional) and serve with more lemon wedges.

Easy and so delicious!

"Honestly, even the big ones only take about 4 minutes total to cook."

THE GAME WINNER!

Playing Virtua Tennis allows you to feel as though you're the next Roger Federer, but it can be challenging. You need good reflexes and keen eyesight to follow the fast-paced action. You see a lobbed shot and you charge the net using your controller. You smash home a blast that wins the match and the game – this is called a game winner! You can celebrate your win, and satisfy your hunger with this dish, which is a great celebratory feast for when you finish your gaming session, or if you want to celebrate with the gaming competition!

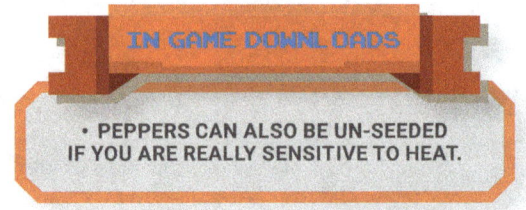

IN GAME DOWNLOADS
- PEPPERS CAN ALSO BE UN-SEEDED IF YOU ARE REALLY SENSITIVE TO HEAT.

INGREDIENTS

10 baby potatoes, halved

2–4 ears husked corn (fresh or frozen)

2 cups cherry or baby tomatoes

1 cup pitted green and/or black olives (I like a mix of both)

2 chili peppers, sliced (with seeds)

1 head of garlic, sliced in half

1 lb muscles (fresh or frozen)

1 lb shrimp, shelled and cleaned

Handful of fresh oregano, basil or parsley or 1 Tbsp dried (oregano works well in this dish but I use a bit of them all)

METHOD

1. Pre heat oven to 425°. Put about ½ cup of olive oil in the bottom of a large roasting pan at least 3 inches deep. Add potatoes, corn, peppers, olives and tomatoes and both halves of the head of garlic in roasting pan (rub the garlic heads all over the potatoes then add to the pan)

2. Salt and pepper everything then place in oven. Cook for 25-30 minutes until potatoes are golden and soft.

3. Take out of oven and add mussels and shrimp and throw herbs over the whole dish.

4. Place in oven again for about 5 minutes until mussels open and shrimp is pink. Throw away any mussels that do not open.

5. Serve with crusty bread and or a green salad! A bit of fresh lemon squeezed on the shellfish makes for a bright note.

Inspired by the video game Virtua Tennis

THE KID AGAINST THE WIND & WINNING THE STANLEY CUP!

IT'S the late 70s to mid 80s. My four closest friends each have gaming systems. My friend John has the Atari 2600, my friend Brad has the Intellivision and my friends Greg and Doug, the twins, were fortunate enough to have the more expensive Colecovision system. I don't have a system of my own but that doesn't matter. My friends and I spend weekends going from one house to another, playing games.

> "WHAT ELSE COULD A KID GAMER ASK FOR? WELL, MAYBE TO WIN THE STANLEY CUP?"

When not gaming we spend hours arguing over who is the best gamer. Occasionally, we have sleepover marathons where we stay up all night playing video games and joking around. Marathon highlights include pizza bites, bags of pretzels and chips provided by my friends' mothers.

During one of these marathons I'm playing football on my friend Brad's system while his older brother watches on. I was never really good at playing the football game and Brad nearly always beat me. I went for a play, one that he was always seemingly ready for, but this time I controlled myself and snuck in the code. Brad was predicting a run play, when I actually called for a pass play. He was totally caught off-guard, not only because I caught the ball and started running, but then went on to actually score a touchdown. As I was making my player run, I heard (and still do to this day), his brother calling out, "The kid against the wind!" To me it was a sweet gaming moment that I savored for all of one more play, because Brad went on to beat me.

Good games, good food and good friends, what else could a kid gamer ask for?

Well, maybe to win the Stanley Cup? It's the 1973-74 season, the first time the Flyers won the Stanley Cup, and I'm ten years old. One of the volunteers in the swimming area at Wiedener Memorial School in Philly was related to Flyers management and made a bet with me. If I swam one lap in the school's pool without help, he'd get the team to bring the cup to our school. Bring it on.

Here's me and the Stanley Cup, proof positive that I swam that lap and was school hero for a day. The original Flyers team all signed their autographs for me to boot.

Check out Breakaway Hockey Chicken Parmesan (p.77) inspired by NHL 2018.

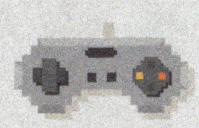

IN GAME DOWNLOADS

- **TRY USING YOUR FAVOURITE BREAKFAST SAUSAGE OR EVEN BACON INSTEAD OF HAM!**
- **TOP WITH YOUR FAVORITE CONDIMENT LIKE SALSA OR HOT SAUCE.**

HIGH OCTANE BREAKFAST HUB CAPS

Heading out for a morning high-octane ride in Forza Horizon 4 with your teammates will be fun, but you're bound to lose unless you start the day with these delicious breakfast hubcaps. This recipe makes 12 breakfast hub caps and can feed up to 6 of your fast-driving gamer friends. They're quick to make and will have you fully fueled for more racing fun in no time!

Inspired by the video game Forza Horizon 4

0:15 PREP TIME

0:45 COOK TIME

6 SERVINGS

INGREDIENTS

- 1 package Ore-Ida shredded hash brown potatoes
- ¼ large onion, diced
- ¼ bell pepper, diced
- 8 oz shredded mozzarella cheese
- 1 large ham steak, diced
- 1 dozen large eggs
- Salt and pepper

METHOD

1. Preheat oven to 400°. Spray a cupcake pan (medium sized 12 cupcake pan) with non-stick spray and press ¼ cup shredded potatoes into each cup of the pan. Make sure to press up on all sides of the cupcake hole.

2. Bake for 20 minutes until potatoes are set. Let cool completely.

3. Preheat oven to 350°. Add diced ham, onion, pepper and 1 egg and some cheese into each tin. Use a fork to ensure cheese runs throughout the tin.

4. Bake for 45 minutes or until egg is set and cheese is brown.

5. Use a butter knife to gently loosen each egg hub cap from muffin tins and serve on a plate. Top with your favorite condiment.

RECORDING BOOTH SAUSAGE & PEPPERS

You got the call to voice a character in an upcoming game. You're excited that you have an acting gig that will not only allow you to put food on the table for another week, but also allow you to keep pursuing your passion of acting! You have the character information the game developers have provided in your hand, but you need a little time to digest the information before heading into the recording booth to record the lines. Why not satisfy yourself and your fellow voice actors with a steaming hot sausage and pepper sandwich while running over the lines? These sandwiches are easy to make and will be gone before the voice director calls "Action"!

0:05 PREP TIME

0:20 COOK TIME

8 SERVINGS

INGREDIENTS

- 1 lb sweet peppers, any color (try brighter colors for summer!)
- 2 large yellow onions (can also be Vidalia onions, if you prefer mild onions)
- 3–4 Tbsp olive oil
- ¼ tsp salt (or more for taste)
- 2 lb of your favorite sausage, bratwurst or other fresh sausage

METHOD

1. Slice onions and peppers roughly.

2. Pour olive oil into pan and heat over medium heat. Once oil is hot, add green peppers and onions. Turn onions and peppers occasionally until the onions and peppers begin to get tender (about 5 to 10 minutes).

3. Add sausages to pan and cook for another 8 to 10 minutes, turning sausages frequently to allow even cooking.

4. Serve sausage and onions on a plate to have a low-carb meal, or pile 1 sausage with onions and peppers onto a lightly toasted bun and enjoy!

IN GAME DOWNLOADS

- IF YOU PREFER A GRILLED TASTE, TRY GRILLING EVERYTHING INSTEAD OF PAN-FRYING. SIMPLY USE A CHARCOAL OR GAS GRILL, GRILL THE VEGETABLES IN A GRILL BASKET FOR 10 TO 12 MINUTES UNTIL EDGES OF VEGETABLES ARE BROWN, THEN MOVE VEGETABLES TO THE COOLER SIDE OF THE GRILL AND PUT THE SAUSAGES ON THE HOT SIDE FOR 8 TO 10 MINUTES, FLIPPING OCCASIONALLY. SERVE AND ENJOY!

HAIL TO THE KING HAMBURGERS

Duke Nukem is one big badass. Taking out the bad guys, freeing babes from certain alien horrors, and doing it with style! He's been doing it for nearly 25 years. But how does Duke keep his energy up? Simple – with one of his mighty Duke Burgers! After developing this recipe, they became an overnight sensation. So much so, that he started his own burger franchise, aptly named Duke Burgers. You can visit Duke Burgers while playing Duke Nukem Anniversary or make them yourself with this jacked-up burger recipe! Hail to the king, baby! Serve these up to 2 really hungry bad asses so they can get out there and take out the alien scum.

0:07 PREP TIME

0:14 COOK TIME

2 SERVINGS

INGREDIENTS

- 1 lb lean ground beef (80% lean works well)
- 1 package of onion soup mix
- 1 Tbsp McCormick Montreal Steak seasoning
- 1 tsp spicy brown mustard
- 2 slices sandwich cheese
- 1 tsp diced jalapeño

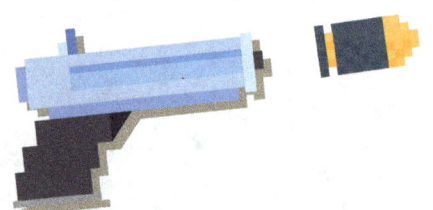

METHOD

1. In a large bowl mix ground beef, spices, seasonings and mustard together. Split into 2 equal parts, then take about half of the meat mixture and start to form a patty.

2. Take 1 slice of cheese and break into 4 equal pieces and stack together and put on top of 1st patty. Take 2nd portion of the meat and place on top of the first patty and form into 1 whole patty. Repeat for 2nd portion of meat. You should have 2 identical burger patties at this point. Wrap burger patties in aluminum foil and place into refrigerator until ready to cook.

3. To cook burgers, spray non-stick pan with cooking spray and heat to medium low. Wait until pan is hot enough to make a drop of water dance, then put burgers on. Let cook for 7 minutes per side for medium/well. Take off pan and let rest for 2 minutes to let juices redistribute, then put onto a lightly toasted hamburger bun or Kaiser roll. Top with your favorite toppings. Go hog wild with the combinations and enjoy!

Inspired by the video game Duke Nukem 3D

IN GAME DOWNLOADS

• BURGERS CAN ALSO BE COOKED IN AN OVEN! PRE-HEAT OVEN TO 425°, THEN COOK BURGERS 15 MINUTES PER SIDE FOR WELL DONE OR 12 MINUTES FOR MEDIUM/WELL. PLACE ANOTHER SLICE OF CHEESE ON TOP 2 MINUTES BEFORE 2ND FLIP IS DONE TO ENSURE CHEESE MELTS WELL ONTO THE BURGER.

• ALSO TRY DIFFERENT SPICE BLENDS LIKE TACO SEASONING AND DIFFERENT TYPES OF CHEESES FOR UNIQUE FLAVORS THAT WILL HAVE YOUR GAMING FRIENDS SAY YOU'RE "GROOVY"!

PLAYING THE PART
CALL OF DUTY: INFINITE WARFARE

I WAS cast to play Captain Maureen Ferran in the 2016 game Call of Duty: Infinite Warfare. I have to be totally honest, I had no idea it was a MoCap job when I booked it. I had never done motion capture before, so it was completely different experience from your regular run of the mill voice gig.

The writer, Brian Bloom, was also the star of the game and I also worked on it with Claudia Black (FarScape, Stargate-SG 1) and surprisingly, David "The Hoff" Hasselhoff from Baywatch and Knight Rider.

The major difference with MoCap and regular VO (voice over) gigs is that you have to memorize your lines! Just like a regular acting gig you also have to hit your mark (move to the required place while delivering line) and do all of the actions that your character does. In a nutshell it's plain old TV or film acting only you're wearing a motion capture suit which consists of black tight trousers, black tight top, black running shoes or boots and a skull cap with dozens of insect antennas sprouting from your head. The entire getup is covered with fuzzy little dots so the various digital cameras can track and capture your motion, hence the name.

I have to admit, I never quite felt comfortable in the suit. For me, costume helps me become the character, especially if it's a military uniform. It helps me find the posture, bearing and weight. I don't think Ivanova (Babylon 5) would have been as easy to inhabit if I was wearing a leotard with polka dots all over it!

In any event it was a terrific experience and one for the books. Here's a fun recipe inspired by Call of Duty: Infinite Warfare, enjoy!

IN GAME DOWNLOADS

- YOU CAN MAKE THE WHOLE THING VEGETARIAN JUST LEAVE OUT THE CHICKEN AND ADD MORE SLICED, GRILLED OR SAUTÉED VEGGIES, OR MAKE IT VEGAN BY USING VEGGIES AND VEGAN CHEESE.
- YOU CAN ADD MORE OR LESS SPICE.

CAPTAIN FERRAN'S ON-THE-GO CHICKEN WRAPS

Captain Maureen Ferran has been called in to investigate a potential secret weapons deployment on Europa. Our heroine and the captain team up to further investigate and eliminate the potentially lethal weapon from making it to Earth to finish the assault the SDF had begun in Geneva. Ferran was the Commanding Officer of the S.A.T.O. Tigris DDX, one of only two ships left operational after the SDF's sneak attack on the UNSA fleet over Geneva. Ferran disobeyed orders from Admiral Raines and jumped back into the area to search for them, saving both their lives at great personal risk to herself and her crew, showing her dedication to her comrades. When not risking life and limb for others, Captain Ferran enjoys fast and delicious chicken wraps.

0:05 PREP TIME

0:12 COOK TIME

4-8 SERVINGS

INGREDIENTS

- 4 large flour or gluten-free tortillas
- 2–3 grilled chicken breasts, sliced thinly
- 1 cup good quality jarred or homemade marinara sauce
- 2–3 cups shredded mozzarella
- 1 cup grated Parmesan cheese
- ½ cup grilled vegetables, like bell peppers or zucchini*
- ¾ cup chopped cherry tomatoes*
- ½ cup torn fresh basil leaves or 1 tsp dried Italian seasoning
- ½ tsp red chili flakes
- 2–3 Tbsp extra-virgin olive oil

*veggies are optional

METHOD

1. Spread a thin layer of marinara onto each tortilla. Top with chicken, mozzarella, Parmesan, chili flakes, cherry tomatoes, veggies (if using) and basil.

2. Tightly fold the edges of the large tortilla towards the center, creating pleats. After wrapping tightly, flip it around so the folds are on the bottom and they stick together.

3. In a large nonstick skillet, heat a very thin layer of olive oil over medium-high heat. Add two chicken wraps, folded side down, and cook until golden, about 3 minutes. Flip and cook until golden on the other side, about 3 minutes more. You can also do one at a time if that's more comfortable for you, use a medium size pan if that's the case.

4. Remove from heat and repeat with remaining wraps adding more olive oil to the pan when necessary.

5. Sprinkle more Parmesan on top, if desired, and then slice into wedges. Serve warm.

Inspired by the video game Call of Duty: Infinite Warfare

HACK ATTACK!

WRAP HACKS

A sandwich made with two slices of bread and a spread? Too much bread, not enough filling. An open-faced sandwich solves the problem but is messy as hell to eat and if you have a game control in your hand, that dog won't hunt. This is why I love tortillas. They now have everything from corn to whole wheat to gluten-free and rice tortillas, something for everyone!

I smear some mustard and mayo or soft cheese like goat cheese, ricotta or an herb blend ready-made spreadable cheese on a tortilla, then start layering yummy ingredients.

Make a BLT wrap with mayo, crispy bacon, avocado, sliced romaine and baby tomatoes with a dash of hot sauce. Make a spicy chicken salad wrap, an Italian "sub" wrap with fire-roasted peppers and marinated artichokes, salami, sliced black olives and some mayonnaise mixed with ricotta cheese or shredded mozzarella or even a dash of your favorite Italian salad dressing.

Wraps are also a great way to use up leftovers, heck I've even made a potato salad and ham wrap and it was delicious.

Smoked salmon, scrambled eggs and cream cheese wrap with dill is a favorite of mine and of course the "breakfast burrito" is a dish I have had from just about every catering truck on a film or TV set I have ever worked on! You can wrap or fold, slice or not, all up to you!

Make sure you slice the wraps in half at an angle, so you can see the fillings better and it's easier to eat or cut into thick pinwheels to share with friends. If you want to keep your hands clean simply wrap it in wax paper, paper towels or a napkin and keep on playing!

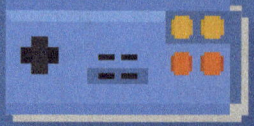

CATCH OF THE DAY TUNA BURGERS

Have you spent hours on the water trying to catch bass in Sega's Bass Fishing, trying to bring in the Big One? Hungry for something that's fresh but not fishy? Try making some Catch of the Day Tuna Burgers and you won't go home empty handed. To quote a famous line, "Keeper Size!" This is enough to feed two gamers – but can be doubled to serve even more of your teammates!

Inspired by the video game Sega Bass Fishing

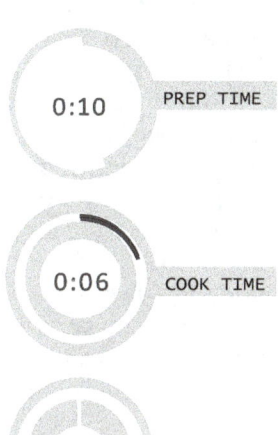

0:10 PREP TIME

0:06 COOK TIME

2 SERVINGS

INGREDIENTS

1½ pounds skinless, boneless tuna
2 tsp Dijon mustard
2 shallots, peeled and cut into chunks
½ cup coarse bread crumbs
1 Tbsp capers, drained
Salt and freshly ground black pepper
2 Tbsp butter or olive oil
Lemon wedges
Tabasco sauce

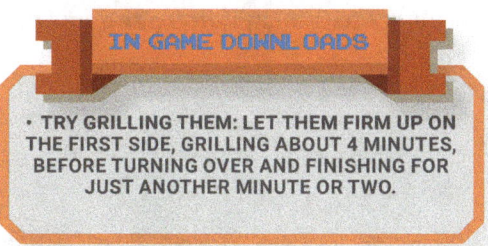

IN GAME DOWNLOADS
- TRY GRILLING THEM: LET THEM FIRM UP ON THE FIRST SIDE, GRILLING ABOUT 4 MINUTES, BEFORE TURNING OVER AND FINISHING FOR JUST ANOTHER MINUTE OR TWO.

METHOD

1. Cut the tuna into large chunks and put about a quarter of it into the container of a food processor, along with the mustard. Turn the machine on, and let it run — stopping to scrape down the sides if necessary — until the mixture becomes pasty.

2. Add the shallots and the remaining tuna and pulse the machine on and off until the fish is chopped and well combined with the puree. No piece should be larger than a quarter inch or so; be careful not make the mixture too fine.

3. Scrape the mixture into a bowl, and by hand, stir in the bread crumbs, capers and some salt and pepper.

4. Shape into four burgers. (You can cover and refrigerate the burgers for a few hours at this point.)

5. Place the butter or oil in a 12-inch nonstick skillet and turn the heat to medium-high. When the butter foam subsides, or the oil is hot, cook the burgers for 2 to 3 minutes a side, turning once. To check for doneness, make a small cut and peek inside. Be careful not to overcook. Serve on a bed of greens or on buns or by themselves, with lemon wedges and Tabasco or any dressing you like.

HOP ALONG ENCHILADAS

Chickens aren't the only animals tempting fate by trying to cross busy, congested highways; frogs have also gotten into the act, in attempt to satisfy their adrenaline urge! In the game Frogger, you have to maneuver your adventurous frog safely to his little lily pad – which happens to be across a dangerous road, with treacherous speeding cars and precariously careening floating logs. You'll be burning up calories trying to get all of your frogs across, so when you and your gamer friends get hungry, try making some of these enchiladas to keep in the fridge for a fast meal that is sure to satisfy everyone in your game party. Since it's made with store-bought rotisserie chicken, this recipe is a snap to make and serve up!

0:10 PREP TIME

0:30 COOK TIME

6-8 SERVINGS

INGREDIENTS

1 whole rotisserie chicken with all the meat picked off and shredded
16–18 small tortillas
2 cans of your favorite enchilada sauce*
4 oz cream cheese, softened
8 oz shredded cheese, divided into two equal portions.
1 small onion diced finely (optional)

* You can also use one can of enchilada sauce and a can/jar taco sauce.

METHOD

1. Pre-heat oven to 350°. In a large mixing bowl, put shredded chicken meat, onions and ⅓ of the sauce and ½ of the cheese and mix well.

2. Put a thin layer of the sauce into a baking dish – just enough to coat the bottom. Spread 1 teaspoon of cream cheese onto a tortilla, then fill tortilla with some of the chicken mix and roll up and place into the baking dish – seam-side down to ensure enchilada stays rolled up while baking. Repeat tortilla filling method until all tortillas are filled and in baking dish.

3. Cover the entire dish of enchiladas with sauce and bake for 45 minutes. Figure on serving 2 to 3 enchiladas per gamer in your party.

Inspired by the Atari 2600 video game Frogger

IN GAME DOWNLOADS

- I BUY 2 OR 3 CHICKENS AT A TIME, PICK ALL THE MEAT. IF YOU HAVE A VACUUM SEALER, YOU CAN SEAL IT AND FREEZE IT. THE MEAT WILL KEEP FOR MONTHS IN THE FREEZER! THEN YOU'LL HAVE A PACKET IN YOUR FREEZER WHEN YOU WANT TO MAKE MORE ENCHILADAS!

IN GAME DOWNLOADS

- TRY USING SOME ADDITIONAL VEGGIES IN YOUR SANDWICH LIKE MUSHROOMS TO GIVE THE SANDWICH EVEN MORE FLAVOR!

THE PHILLY SPECIAL CHEESESTEAK

It's been 58 years in the making, but the Philadelphia Eagles have finally won the Superbowl title. The last time they won a championship was before there was such a thing as the Superbowl! If there's one play that will be remembered throughout football history, that play would be the one the Eagles called late in the game, called – fittingly enough, The Philly Special. There's no doubt that this play will now be in the list of plays for the upcoming pro football videogames! To honor my favorite football team, and to celebrate my Philly pride, I am including my latest yummy recipe, aptly named The Philly Special Cheesesteak. This may look like your typical cheesesteak, but like the name implies, this one is special! Try this one out if you want a memorable cheesesteak!

0:15 PREP TIME

0:20 COOK TIME

3 SERVINGS

INGREDIENTS

4 oz link of kielbasa
½ large onion, sliced
1 medium green pepper, sliced
1 slice of cheese per sandwich
Long hoagie roll per sandwich
¼ tsp salt
⅛ tsp pepper
2 Tbsp olive oil

METHOD

1. Put kielbasa in freezer for roughly 20 minutes to firm up a bit and to keep from overheating in the food processor. Remove and run through food processor with its shredding blade attached. Once done place kielbasa into refrigerator to keep cool until ready to cook.

2. Sautee onions and green peppers in a large skillet with oil for 10 minutes. Salt and pepper the vegetables, and heat until tender.

3. Remove veggies from pan and place kielbasa meat into skillet with a little more vegetable spray or oil to help brown meat. Cook for roughly 5 to 10 minutes, stirring and tossing throughout so meat won't burn or stick to pan.

4. Remove from skillet and put into roll, along with vegetables and top with a slice of cheese. Serve and enjoy.

Inspired by the video game Madden 2019

HACK ATTACK!

ONE PAN MEALS

A few thoughts on quick meals and the idea of "not having enough time" to cook.

I recall a few years back when Julia Child caught flack for pronouncing that everybody should use fresh produce all the time. Many people, rightfully, argued that a lot of people did not have access to or could not afford fresh produce and that she was being rather naïve or "entitled" when making that statement, so I want to preface this hack with a disclaimer of my own (to avoid flack and outrage).

I know you're busy and I know people with two-career families, multiple day jobs, and children are stressed out to the max and that fast food or something out of the freezer or can is sometimes all you can do, but... there are easy ways to throw a great, healthy meal together in less time than it takes for the Kung Pao chicken and Chow Mein to arrive. Let's talk about one dish wonders a bit more. I've talked a bit about soups and such but here's a really easy planning technique:

Start with a decent sized roasting pan and begin with the bottom layer. You can choose potatoes, sweet potatoes, squash, cabbage, sliced carrots or any other firm vegetable. Make sure you cut them in a similar size so that they cook evenly, otherwise the little misshapen ones will burn. Make sure you coat them all with oil then season with salt and pepper

and add some garlic gloves or shallots and some herbs if using. Roast that at 425° for about 20-30 minutes until they are tender.

At this point you can take the pan out. Make sure the bottom layer is browned on the underside. Flip them, I use a thin flexible spatula for this. Add another veggie or tomato layer like spinach, kale or thinly sliced onions, zucchini, baby tomatoes, baby vegetables cut in half, broccolini, asparagus etc.

> "*But... there are easy ways to throw a great, healthy meal together in less time than it takes for the Kung Pao Chicken and Chow Mein to arrive.*"

that you have tossed in oil and seasoned.

Then on top of that you can put a protein layer: fish like sea bass, salmon, trout, or shrimp, poultry like chicken tenders or sliced chicken breast, or even sausages (I would brown them in a pan before adding).

The possibilities are endless! Cook that for about 10-20 minutes until the protein is cooked.

Finally, add another flavor layer of something perky like feta cheese and pepperoncini, capers or a drizzle of pesto or your favorite marinara sauce or even vinaigrette and another handful of fresh herbs. Then serve.

It sounds time consuming but it's really not, you're only taking the pan out twice; once to add the protein and then when it's finished! You can do pretty much everything in the pan itself.

You can make this fun for everyone by having a consensus as to what goes in the pan or even a challenge by trying to use as many ingredients as the fridge provides. Some one-pan meals might turn out to be your new "go to" favorites. I made one with savoy cabbage and halibut that I thought would be a little dodgy but turned out to be very nice indeed!

The message here is that with a little bit of effort you can make a homemade meal very quickly. In fact, if you have a few minutes before you go to work or the night before you can prep the veggies and put them in an airtight container in the fridge.

Another way I love to use random "one off" veggies and potato is to make a tart with no crust. Just butter a round tart pan and layer thinly sliced, olive oil coated (and seasoned with salt and pepper) potato, zucchini, tomato, peppers, squash... whatever you have. I put them in a nice concentric circle like a fruit tart, then cover in foil and bake at 400° for 15-20 minutes then remove foil, scatter some parmesan and Kalamata, or other briny olives on top then bake for another 15-20 minutes until the veggies are soft and the top browned. Let rest for 5-10 minutes then sprinkle with fresh basil, thyme, and parsley and serve. It's also nice at room temperature. This is a great vegetarian dish that can be made vegan by substituting vegan "butter" or olive oil to coat the dish and vegan "cheese" on top.

VFX POWER SLOPPY JOES

You and your girlfriend are enjoying a good video game when suddenly, an evil mastermind jumps out of your video game and snatches your girlfriend from you and carries her off into a comic book-style video game. Time for a VFX powerup by way of these fast and delicious sloppy joe sandwiches! This recipe makes enough for up to 4 superhero players.

Inspired by the video game Viewtiful Joe

0:10 PREP TIME

1:06 COOK TIME

4 SERVINGS

INGREDIENTS

2 Tbsp olive oil
1 cup finely diced onion
1 tsp minced garlic
2 lb lean ground beef
1 tsp tomato paste
2¾ cups tomato puree
½ tsp chili powder
½ tsp Tabasco sauce
1 tsp pureed canned chipotle in adobo
1 bay leaf
4 kaiser rolls or hamburger buns
4 slices cheddar cheese (optional)

METHOD

1. In a large skillet over medium heat add oil and sauté onions until translucent, about 5 to 6 minutes. Add garlic, and sauté for another 30 seconds, then add ground beef, and sauté until well browned, 15 to 20 minutes.

2. Add tomato paste, tomato puree, chili powder, Tabasco, chipotle and bay leaf. Stir until blended. Raise heat to bring to a boil, then reduce heat to low. Simmer mixture, stirring occasionally, until thick enough to spread on a sandwich, about 45 minutes.

3. To serve, toast the buns and put about ½ cup onto the bottom of each roll, and top with cheddar cheese to taste. Return bottom halves to the broiler until cheese just melts, or microwave bottom bun with meat mixture for 30 seconds, then top with the remaining halves and enjoy.

IN GAME DOWNLOADS

- YOU CAN ALSO SUBSTITUTE YOUR FAVORITE HOT SAUCE INSTEAD OF TOBASCO SAUCE. TRY DIFFERENT CHEESES FOR A DIFFERENT FLAVOR; TRY SMOKED MOZZARELLA OR EVEN PEPPER JACK CHEESE!

DRAGON POWER MAC & CHEESE

Spyro has been busy trying to save his fellow dragons from the evil Gnasty Gnorc, who has vowed to rid the realms of dragons once and for all. Even a small, sleek dragon like Spyro needs something to help him keep flapping and spitting flames. What could be better than a nice bowl of Dragon Power Mac & Cheese? This recipe makes enough for you and a friend to enjoy while helping Spyro in his quest.

0:02 PREP TIME

0:12 COOK TIME

2 SERVINGS

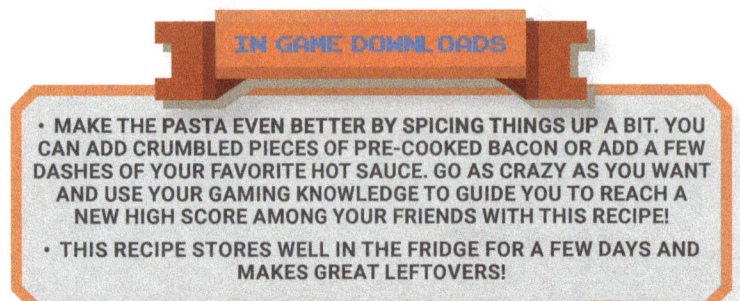

IN GAME DOWNLOADS

- MAKE THE PASTA EVEN BETTER BY SPICING THINGS UP A BIT. YOU CAN ADD CRUMBLED PIECES OF PRE-COOKED BACON OR ADD A FEW DASHES OF YOUR FAVORITE HOT SAUCE. GO AS CRAZY AS YOU WANT AND USE YOUR GAMING KNOWLEDGE TO GUIDE YOU TO REACH A NEW HIGH SCORE AMONG YOUR FRIENDS WITH THIS RECIPE!
- THIS RECIPE STORES WELL IN THE FRIDGE FOR A FEW DAYS AND MAKES GREAT LEFTOVERS!

INGREDIENTS

1 lb elbow macaroni

12 oz sharp cheddar or white cheese

3 tsp unsalted butter

8 oz cream cheese, cut into 1-inch pieces

2 cups milk

Salt

METHOD

1. Cook pasta in big pot of salted water until barely al dente then drain.

2. While pasta is cooking, brink milk to a simmer in another large pot (large enough to hold pasta when cooked). Reduce milk to low then add cream cheese and whisk until smooth. Add the cheddar cheese and butter - whisk until completely melted. Season with a good amount of salt and pepper.

3. Add pasta to cheesy mixture. Stir to coat all of the pasta - about 2 to 3 minutes. Season again with more salt and pepper.

Inspired by the video game Spyro the Dragon

ARTHUR'S SPICY ASIAN MEAT BUNS WITH BOK CHOY SLAW

In Shining the Holy Ark, you play the role of the mercenary Arthur as he travels with his companions in order to capture the renegade ninja Rodi and return him to the king who has charged you with this hazardous mission. Along the way you have to defeat magical beasts and other obstacles. This mission may take a while, so you and your RPG friends will need plenty of energy to keep going. Try making some of these spicy meat buns with bok choy slaw, and you'll have plenty of energy to spare while exploring!

0:10 PREP TIME

0:06 COOK TIME

4 SERVINGS

INGREDIENTS

½ cup hoisin sauce
4 tsp chili-based sauce, such as sambal oelek, Sriracha or garlic chili sauce
5 Tbsp white or rice vinegar
1 bell pepper (seeded), cut into strips about ¼ inch
1 small head of bok choy, stems sliced thinly, and leaves reserved
1 lb ground pork, chicken or turkey
3–4 Tbsp mayonnaise
4 split top hot dog buns
½ cup of fresh herbs like mint, basil and cilantro
Salt and pepper to taste

Inspired by the video game Shining The Holy Ark

METHOD

1. Stir the hoisin, chili sauce and one tablespoon of vinegar together in a bowl.

2. In another bowl combine bell pepper, bok choy stems and remaining vinegar, season to taste with salt and pepper.

3. Cook meat in a non-stick pan over medium high heat. Season with salt and pepper and stir and break up until it is beginning to brown (5–6 minutes) add ¼ cup of the hoisin mixture, cook about a minute until meat is coated.

4. Spread mayonnaise on buns then line with the bok choy leaves, add meat, slaw and remaining hoisin mixture and fresh herbs. Serve with more hot sauce if desired.

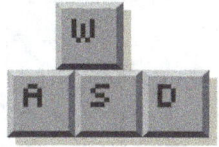

VEGGIES & SIDES

"Creating your veggies is easy when they're tasty! So get creative with your side dishes and create a fun, fabulous meal!"

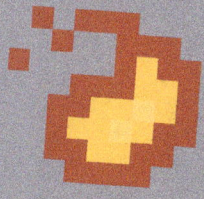

GHOST BUSTING EGGPLANT PARMESAN

Luigi is a man of many talents; plumber, ghost hunter and even an Italian chef! When he's not ghost busting in his large mansion, he enjoys a tasty eggplant parmesan, with a good tomato sauce and lots of bubbly cheese! Why not make some, and then help him vacuum up some more ghosts? This recipe can feed two hungry ghost-busting gamers.

0:10 PREP TIME

1:20 COOK TIME

2 SERVINGS

INGREDIENTS

2 cups plain dry bread crumbs
2 medium eggplants, cut into ¼-inch-thick slices
4 large eggs, beaten
3 Tbsp water
1 (24 oz) jar tomato sauce
½ cup grated Parmesan cheese
6 slices mozzarella cheese

METHOD

1. Beat eggs with water to make egg wash. Dip eggplant disks into eggs and then bread crumbs, place on baking sheet.

2. Bake eggplant for 25 minutes, flipping halfway.

3. Spray 9x13-inch pan with cooking spray then pour 1 cup tomato sauce into bottom of pan. Arrange eggplant into baking dish, cover with tomato sauce and parmesan cheese. Cover with foil and bake for 45 minutes.

4. Take foil off and place mozzarella cheese on top and bake uncovered for another 10 minutes until cheese is bubbly and golden. Remove from oven and serve over your favorite pasta or with crusty bread!

Inspired by the video game Luigi's Haunted Mansion

HACK ATTACK!

HELLO HALO!

Sometimes I'm working on games simultaneously, as some require multiple recording sessions. Unfortunately I was doing World of Warcraft and at the same time I booked Halo 4. I'm billed as voice or additional voices on Halo, so unlike my friend Cas Anvar who had a lead in the game, I am just an extra. Nonetheless, it's a great credit. Extra points if you can discover who I played in the game!

I love my healthy bowls and you can make it your own with a variety of ingredients.

The basic recipe is this:

1. Start with a grain or starch:

Quinoa, barley, Israeli couscous, brown, white or wild rice, faro, beans, roasted potatoes or sweet potatoes, even oatmeal can be savory.

2. Add your favorite veggies or salad greens for crunch:

Tomatoes, cucumbers, avocado, onions, peppers, cooked asparagus, broccoli or zuccinni (this is where leftovers come into play... shredded cabbage, etc).

3. Add an animal protein if you want:

Tuna, hard boiled or soft-boiled egg, left over chicken or fish or beef or pork.

4. Add nuts or seeds, and dried or fresh fruit: Blueberries go great with chicken, walnuts and goat cheese believe it or not.

5. Think of a theme: Asian? Mexican? Breakfast bowl? Sweet and savory?

6. Add some fun fermented items if you're into that (I am!):

Kimchi or some pickled vegetables.

7. To dairy or not to dairy?

Some people like to add a scoop of cottage cheese or diced or grated or crumbled cheese or even plain yogurt.

8. Add some fresh herbs or spices if you want:

I love basil leaves and Italian parsley leaves in my bowls or if it's a spicy bowl I load on the hot sauce and spicy pickled veggies like a Taqueria mix.

Layer the bowl however you like it and dress every layer or simply add dressing at the end. You can use coleslaw and potato salad, whatever you want.

One of my favorites is left over faro which has been cooked in apple cider with a bayleaf and salt with cubes of chicken and avocado sitting on a bed of dressed field greens with a handful of crumbled goat cheese or blue cheese and some raw walnuts and chopped apple on top. YUM!

My Asian bowl is brown rice with a bit of soy sauce and sesame oil mixed in, some left over salmon pieces and a bit of avocado, cubed cucumber for crunch and some spicy Sriracha sauce mixed with grated ginger and soy sauce and sesame oil drizzled over it. Fast, healthy and delicious!

I also love cooked quinoa with steamed spinach or baby kale with a poached egg or two on top and a simple dressing made of olive oil, lemon juice and salt and pepper.

If you have some BBQ ingredients left over make a grilled steak and pepper bowl over rice or beans with a squirt of BBQ sauce mixed with mayonnaise or olive oil and a splash of vinegar for punch. Throw some herbs or more veggies in there and enjoy!

Use your imagination... and use your leftovers!

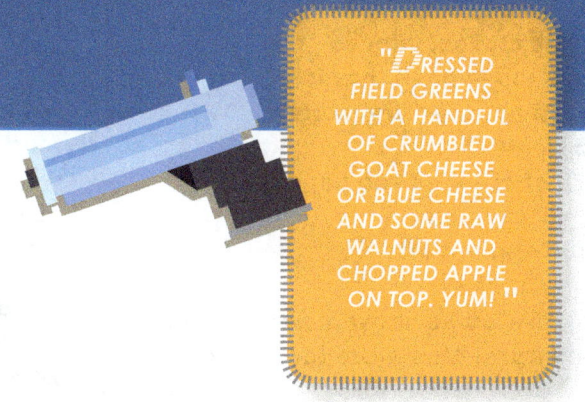

"*Dressed field greens with a handful of crumbled goat cheese or blue cheese and some raw walnuts and chopped apple on top. Yum!*"

SPORTY CALIFORNIA EASY ZUCCHINI PASTA

You and your gaming crew have gotten together for your weekly gaming session and you're set for some rowdy, raucous gaming fun. There quite a few hungry gamers in this group, but you don't want to get weighed down by burgers and fries – tonight you want something that will fill you up, but still let you move fast enough to keep up with tonight's game of the week; California Games for the Atari 2600. While you're shredding the waves or sidewalks in California games, you can also enjoy this wonderful pasta!

Inspired by the video game California Games

0:10 PREP TIME

0:30 COOK TIME

4-6 SERVINGS

INGREDIENTS

1 small onion, finely diced or thinly sliced depending on your taste
2 lb zucchini, sliced into ¼-inch-thick pieces (for larger zucchini, cut in half lengthwise before slicing)
Salt and pepper
2 garlic cloves, minced
2 cups loose basil leaves
1 lb ziti or other dry pasta
8 oz ricotta
Pinch of crushed red pepper
Zest of 1 lemon
Juice from lemon
6 Tbsp olive oil
1 cup grated Parmesan, pecorino or a mixture, plus more for serving

METHOD

1. Put a large pot of salted water on to boil for the pasta.

2. In a large skillet over medium-high heat, cook the onions in about 3 tablespoons olive oil until softened, 5 to 8 minutes, do not brown them just cook until soft and translucent.

3. Add zucchini, season with salt and pepper and the red pepper flakes, continue cooking, stirring occasionally until soft, about 10 minutes. Remove from heat.

4. Mix garlic, basil and a little salt into a rough paste (use a mortar and pestle or a mini food processor or just mash as well as you can with whatever you have, the back of a large spoon works). You can also chop the whole lot if that's easier for you. Stir in 3 tablespoons olive oil.

5. Add pasta to boiling water. Boil per package instructions but make sure to keep pasta a little undercooked (al dente, which means "to the tooth" for you linguists).

IN GAME DOWNLOADS

- IF YOU DO NOT HAVE OR LIKE ZUCCHINI THEN USE ASPARAGUS OR YELLOW OR SUMMER SQUASH OR A COMBINATION OF VEGETABLES.

6. Drain pasta, reserving 1 cup of cooking water. VERY IMPORTANT! Save that cup of cooking water! You can also use good quality or homemade chicken or vegetable stock for this step of the recipe (handy if you accidently throw the pasta water out).

7. Add cooked pasta to zucchini in skillet and turn heat to medium-high.

8. Add ½ cup cooking water, then the ricotta and lemon zest, check seasoning and adjust. Cook for 1 minute more. Mixture should look creamy.

9. Add a little more pasta water if necessary. Add the basil paste and lemon juice then add half the grated cheese and quickly stir to incorporate.

10. Spoon pasta into bowls and sprinkle with more cheese if you want. Enjoy immediately! I like to serve this with a green salad and crusty warm bread.

IN GAME DOWNLOADS

- INSTEAD OF CHIVES, TRY ADDING SOME GREEN ONIONS OR PERHAPS EVEN MILD ONIONS INTO THE POTATO MASH BEFORE RETURNING TO BAKE.

BORN TO GRILL TWICE-BAKED POTATOES

Hogs of War is a wacky time-based strategy/battle game which pits teams of little hogs against one another for supremacy of the battlefield. With each move your team of plucky little pigs use funny weapons and even funnier dialogue. While you square off with your friends in this classic Playstation game, you'll want to have something that's equally loaded with flavor and substance. Try making these twice-baked potatoes for you and your gaming friends. You can make as many as you want in practically no time, and serve them up with a line from the game, "This potato is for you!" Your friends will gobble them up and you will all be ready for the next round of battle!

0:10 PREP TIME

1:10 COOK TIME

2–4 SERVINGS

INGREDIENTS

2–4 large baking potatoes
Olive oil
2–4 Tbsp sour cream
2 Tbsp chopped chives
¼ cup shredded cheddar cheese
Salt and pepper

METHOD

1. Preheat oven to 425°. Wash and scrub potatoes and dry with paper towels really well. Rub olive oil on potatoes.

2. Prick each potato twice with a fork to allow steam to vent in potatoes. Cook for 1 hour.

3. After 1 hour, take potatoes out and slice in half. Hull out halves with a spoon, leaving some of the potato flesh inside, to allow the skins to maintain their shapes.

4. Mash hulled-out potato flesh with sour cream, chives, salt and pepper until creamy. Place back into potato hulls and top with a pinch of cheese.

5. Bake for another 10 minutes until cheese is melted and enjoy.

Inspired by the video game Hogs of War

VOICE ACTOR PROFILE
CAS ANVAR

CAS Anvar and I worked together on the Halo franchise. He's a multi-talented, award-winning actor who has over one-hundred credits to his name in both film and television. He's currently starring in Amazon Prime's sci-fi epic The Expanse. In a myriad of diverse characters, he plays the Martian fighter pilot with a Texan drawl. Cas also appears in the FX sci-fi hit, The Strain, with Robin Atkin Downes (featured on p.87). Gamers know Cas' incredible range as a voice actor and his Assassins Creed alter ego: Altair. At conventions he often cosplay's Altair (watch out for the hidden blade strapped to his arm!). Anvar is in The Operative with Martin Freeman and Diane Kruger and appears in Lost as Naveen Andrews' brother. He was also our favorite villain, the nefarious Sanjay Desal, on Guillermo Del Toro's The Strain. When he's not working, Cas Anvar enjoys playing paintball with his team, The Suave Bastards, and buzzing around in their custom-made tank called The Mighty Bastard.

CLAUDIA: Since this is a gaming cookbook, I have to ask: do you play any games? If so, which ones?

CAS: Hell yeah I do! I been a hard core gamer since... God... I'm not gonna date myself... but since the beginning. I'm a huge RPG fan, not so big on shooters. My faves are Skyrim (and that sexy sultry voice of Aela The Huntress!), Fallout, Mass Effects, Diablo, but I'm not gonna lie... the best game in the world... THE LAST OF US... I cannot wait for TLOU 2!!

CLAUDIA: Yes, Aela was a hoot to play, thanks for the kind words! So Cas, If you were to have friends over to game, what kinds of food and drinks would you serve?

CAS: Kik cola, Mountain Dew (Nerd Nectar) and some avacado on toast.

CLAUDIA: What is your best dish?

CAS: I make a mean porterhouse steak on the BBQ and a great morning omlette. A kick ass salad. Pancakes I got on lockdown as well and there's this one pasta fresca I do once in a while with sundried tomatoes and pesto. That ain't too shabby.

CLAUDIA: Can you recall the first video game you auditioned for? Did you get that gig?

CAS: Yup. Assassins Creed.

CLAUDIA: What was your favorite game to work on and why?

CAS: I'm going to answer Assassins Creed again because the gaming world and mythology is epic and it's an incredible story. Altair, the character I played, is a frickin Legend!

CLAUDIA: What was the most difficult video game voice assignment you had?

CAS: Command and Conquer: Generals. I had to play multiple characters and do a lot of yelling, and switch voices and accents in a short time span. It was fun as heck but challenged the begeezus outta me. From nerdy Indian scientist to three-hundred pound angry, sputtering Russian general.

CLAUDIA: When did you first decide to get involved in voice work?

CAS: I always wanted to do voice work but it's a very exclusive and hard to break into. I finally managed to get work when I moved to LA and have been loving it ever since. It's awesome to be able to wrap my voice around so many different roles. From a Turkish assassin to a red neck Irish soldier in Halo 4 to a screaming Russian general, it's all possible if I can make it real.

CLAUDIA: Which is more difficult, voice acting or on camera acting?

CAS: I love both and they are so different. I think that the vocal skill required in voice acting is quite substantial, so it requires a lot of training and experience, but once you've aquired the skills and broken into the business its actually quite fluid and fun. Film acting is always challenging you with all the logistics involved; action, sound, lighting, blocking and costume, hair and so on. Every film is like the first one in that sense.

CLAUDIA: If you had your pick of games to voice what would be your first choice.

CAS: I would love to do Assassins Creed again, or Skyrim or The Last of Us or Mass Effects or Magic The Gathering. Wow, you know I love any games that have huge epic fantastic worlds and larger than life characters.

CLAUDIA: When you did the voice of Altair La-Ahad in Assassin's Creed: Revelations, what type of research did you have to do to take on the role?

CAS: I voiced Altair in 2012 and when I auditioned for it, it was top secret and the character was called Hussein and the game was called Saharah so that no one knew what they were auditioning for. When I finally found out I had booked the legendary Altair I only had a few days to do research and prepare. So I kind of just winged it, Claudia but I've got to tell you, it was so much fun.

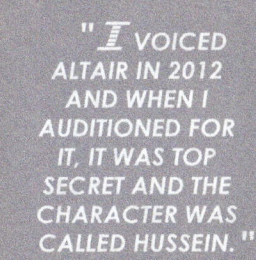

" *I* VOICED ALTAIR IN 2012 AND WHEN I AUDITIONED FOR IT, IT WAS TOP SECRET AND THE CHARACTER WAS CALLED HUSSEIN. "

CAS ANVAR AND NAREN SHANKAR SPEAKING AT THE 2018 WONDERCON, FOR THE EXPANSE.

HACK ATTACK!
BUTTER PORTIONS

Most people enjoy butter, especially on baked potatoes (p.137). If you want more flavor than mere butter alone can provide, you can create a compound butter. Here are some ideas, plus a great hack for how to store it!

SAVORY BUTTERS — try these on vegetables, meats, poultry, fish, seafood, grains and starches:
- garlic, lemon, and tarragon
- rosemary, garlic, red pepper flakes, and anchovy paste
- chives, lemon zest, and shallots,
- smoked paprika, rosemary, thyme, and garlic
- lime juice and finely mince jalapeño
- gorgonzola or blue cheese and parsley
- soy sauce, ginger, garlic, and lime zest
- garlic powder, thyme, salt and pepper
- lemon zest, chives, parsley, salt

SWEET BUTTERS — these are nice on sweet potatoes, rolls, breads, pancakes, corn bread, etc:
- maple syrup and cinnamon
- brown sugar, chopped pecans, and vanilla
- raspberries, powdered sugar, and vanilla
- honey, maple syrup, and nutmeg
- pumpkin spice and brown sugar
- peach compote, vanilla, and sugar
- your favorite jam.

Chop, mince or grate ingredients and mix with softened butter. As a guide, for 1 stick of butter use about 2 Tbsp fresh herbs or 1 tsp dried, and 2 tsp garlic, onion or citrus zest; but there's no need to measure, just experiment until you find a mix you love!

When most people make a batch of compound butter, they simply roll it in parchment paper and plastic wrap. But there's an everyday item you can actually use to place your just-made compound butter and portion it out for later use in your yummy dishes. Simply take an ice cube tray, spray it with cooking spray and then place some of the softened butter mixture into the ice cube receptacles.

Place a piece of plastic wrap, or the ice cube tray lid, over the top, then put the tray into the freezer or fridge to firm up. If you're using the fridge, you should allow at least 8 hours for the butter to really firm up before using. When the butter has fully firmed, you will have evenly-portioned segments of butter to use on whatever you like; fish, steak, in a sauce to add creaminess or whenever you need a perfect pat of butter!

BETA-TESTER BAKED POTATOES

Most people screw up baked potatoes. They either microwave them (the horror!) or they under bake them (one hour at 350°). Enough! Who taught this method? It's antiquated and wrong! The humble potato deserves better, it has been filling us up and nourishing us for a gazillion years, let's show some respect. Try beta-testing my recipe for baked potatoes and you'll see that they're pure perfection. The skin is as crispy as a potato chip and the inside is a moist, gooey, buttery, caramelized, hot joy. You don't even need to serve them with a side. They're great just like this and a perfect diet food to boot when you absolutely need carbs. You can get creative too. Leftover stew? Stick some in a baked potato for a faux meat pie. Some veggie chili in the fridge? Perfect with your potatoes just add a dollop of sour cream and a sprinkle of cheese. we called this dish beta-tester potatoes so go for it, try out all sorts of things. Push the potato to its limits and have fun!

Inspired by video game coding

INGREDIENTS

4 large baking potatoes, like russets
1 Tbsp or more olive oil
Maldon or kosher or other crunchy good salt
FILLINGS:
Butter, sour cream, cheese, herbs, chili, yogurt, soy sauce, hot peppers, pickled vegetables, sauerkraut, mustard, ketchup, salsa, curried mayonnaise and raisins, tuna fish salad, leftovers, heck ANYTHING you want!

METHOD

1. Preheat oven to 425-450°. Scrub potatoes under running water; dry them really well and rub the skin of each with the oil and then sprinkle with salt. If you feel an explosion is possible then pierce the skin of each in three or four places with the tines of a fork. I have never in my life pierced my potatoes and they have never, ever exploded, not once, but I suppose it's the responsible thing for me to write in this recipe ;)

2. Place the potatoes in the oven, and roast for at least 75–120 minutes depending on the size of the potatoes, until they are incredibly crunchy on the outside and fluffy and moist on the inside.

3. Remove the potatoes from the oven (wear an oven mitt), slice them open down the middle, add your choice of filling!

EASY HARVEST CAULIFLOWER STEAKS

You've been playing Harvest Moon on your Super Nintendo system all day, and you have made great progress in restoring the dilapidated farm featured in the game. You've milked all the cows and made sure to feed the chickens, but now you're hungry and need something to help keep you going while playing the game. Why not make some healthy cauliflower steaks? They're easy to make and taste really good! This recipe makes enough for two, and can also be used as a side-dish for those really hungry gamers!

Inspired by the video game Harvest Moon

0:05 PREP TIME

0:40 COOK TIME

2 SERVINGS

INGREDIENTS

1 large whole cauliflower
2–3 Tbsp olive oil
Salt and pepper, to taste
Seasonings

METHOD

1. Preheat oven to 425°. Peel leaves off cauliflower stem. Put cauliflower on a microwave-safe plate with a paper towel and microwave for 5 minutes, turn cauliflower over and microwave again for another 3–4 minutes.

2. Remove carefully from microwave and slice into 1-inch "steaks". If a fleurette breaks off, don't worry about it.

3. Place the cauliflower steaks and fleurettes onto a sheet tray and pour oil over them and season with salt and pepper. Turn them over and repeat. (You can also brush the steaks with oil using a pastry brush).

4. Sprinkle your favorite season on the cauliflower, I like smoked paprika and garlic salt or Berbere seasoning or even fresh herbs or a grilling rub is good on these.

5. Bake cauliflower for 15–30 minutes, flipping steaks to ensure even browning on both sides. Serve as either a vegetarian main meal or side-dish to a protein.

IN GAME DOWNLOADS

- YOU CAN SERVE THIS WITH A SIMPLE DIJON-RED WINE VINAIGRETTE WITH CAPERS, OR CRUMBLING GOAT CHEESE, FETA CHEESE, OLIVES OR EVEN BACON ON TOP AFTER COOKING. IT'S ALSO GREAT JUST ON ITS OWN!

ROASTED PURSUIT WHOLE CAULIFLOWER

You and your gaming friends have been playing a rousing round of Trivial Pursuit Live, and while your brains have been thoroughly stimulated, your taste buds are now in need of the same attention. Pizza and wings? No! Time for a change! Try serving up a vegetable that actaully resembles a brain to boost brainpower!

Inspired by the video game Trivial Pursuit Live

0:15 PREP TIME

1:15 COOK TIME

8 SERVINGS

INGREDIENTS

1 whole head of cauliflower, washed, dried and green leaves removed
2 Tbsp of olive oil
½ tsp salt

FOR VINAIGRETTE DRESSING:
¼ cup olive oil
Juice of half a lemon
2 Tbsp capers (in brine), drained
½ tsp salt
¼ tsp black pepper
large handful (a loose cup or two) of Italian parsley leaves

METHOD

1. Preheat oven to 450°. Place rack in middle of oven.

2. Lightly grease a round or square pan that fits the cauliflower head. Drizzle cauliflower with 2 tablespoons of oil and ½ teaspoon of salt.

3. Bake until tender, about an hour or 1¼ hours. Remove from oven and transfer to a serving dish (you can also serve it in the baking dish but warn people it's hot).

4. Whisk together lemon juice, pepper and capers and remaining ½ teaspoon of salt, then whisk in the remaining ¼ cup of olive oil.

5. Pour dressing over the cauliflower and sprinkle the parsley over the top.

IN GAME DOWNLOADS

- IF YOU DON'T LIKE THE IDEA OF THE CAPER VINAIGRETTE YOU CAN SERVE YOUR ROASTED HEAD OF CAULIFLOWER WITH A LOT OF DIFFERENT THINGS:

- SOFTENED GOAT CHEESE ON THE SIDE IS DELICIOUS –YOU CAN SPRINKLE SOME THYME ON THE CAULIFLOWER BEFORE OR AFTER IT COOKS

- GREEN GODDESS OR BUTTERMILK DRESSING IS ALSO REALLY TASTY.

- YOU CAN SERVE IT PLAIN WITH JUST SALT AND PEPPER.

- PUT GRATED PARMESAN AND FRESH PARSLEY WITH A PINCH OF RED CHILI PEPPER FLAKES ON IT

- I ALSO COOK MY WHOLE HEAD OF CAULIFLOWER STOVE TOP IN TOMATO SAUCE AND BASIL, GARLIC AND SLICED ONIONS (OR JUST MARINARA SAUCE) THEN TOP WITH PARMESAN, IT'S LIKE A HEALTHY "PIZZA"!

- YOU CAN MAKE IT "PUTTANESCA" STYLE BY SAUTÉING ONION AND GARLIC THEN ADDING A CAN OF CHOPPED TOMATOES AND SOME BLACK OLIVES, CAPERS AND CHOPPED UP ANCHOVY FILETS, BASIL AND CHILI FLAKES AND COOK IT STOVE TOP WITH A LID ON THE POT. ADD WATER IF THERE'S NOT ENOUGH LIQUID. WHEN IT'S TENDER IT'S DONE, SPRINKLE WITH PARMESAN AND ENJOY!

RASH AND BASH SUPER ONION

It's just you, your favorite bike and fourteen of your street racing buddies out for a not-so-friendly race along the Nappa Valley Coast. Strap on your helmet because it's a fight to the finish! There's a tasty prize at the end of the race too and it's not the hot biker babes; it's an order of Rash and Bash Super Onions. These tasty treats are better than the ones you can get at a restaurant because you can make them in the oven instead of frying. You can make it and share it or, like a true road rasher, hog the super onion and the glory for yourself.

Inspired by the video game Road Rash

0:10 PREP TIME

0:30 COOK TIME

1-2 SERVINGS

INGREDIENTS

FOR ONION:

1 large sweet onion, such as Vidalia (about 1 lb)
2½ cups all-purpose flour
1 tsp cayenne pepper
2 Tbsp paprika
½ tsp dried thyme
½ tsp dried oregano
½ tsp ground cumin
2½ cups Italian bread crumbs
Freshly ground black pepper
2 large eggs
1 cup whole milk
Kosher salt

METHOD

FOR ONION:

1. Put all dry ingredients (for the onion) in a large bowl and whisk together.

2. Put eggs into a separate bowl and beat until mixed like scrambled egg mix with a splash of milk.

3. Peel onion and remove the bottom roots—but keeping onion intact. Use an apple slicer to slice onion, but do not go all the way through onion. The pieces should fold open like a flower, but not fall completely off of onion.

4. Drop onion into bowl with flower mixture and shake to coat. Remove onion and shake with "petals" facing downward, to remove excess flour.

5. Place onion into egg mixture and roll onion through egg mixture, making sure to coat all "petals" well. Place coated onion into bread crumb mixture and repeat coating.

IN GAME DOWNLOADS

- INSTEAD OF DREDGING THE ONION IN FLOUR THE 2ND TIME, TRY DREDGING IT IN PANKO BREAD CRUMBS OR ITALIAN BREAD CRUMBS.
- FOR A VARIATION ON THE DIP, TRY ADDING A TEASPOON OF HORSERADISH TO THE SAUCE MIX FOR A SPICIER DIPPING SAUCE!
- CAN ALSO BE MADE BY DEEP FRYING. PREHEAT OIL TO 400° AND FRY UNTIL BREADING IS BROWN.

FOR SAUCE:

2 Tbsp mayonnaise
2 Tbsp sour cream
1½ tsp ketchup
½ tsp Worcestershire sauce
¼ tsp paprika
Pinch of cayenne pepper
Kosher salt and freshly ground black pepper

6. Once this has been done, shake excess flour off and put onto a small plate or sheet and place into refrigerator for about an hour, to allow flour to adhere to the onion well.

7. Preheat oven to 400°. Place coated onion onto a lined baking sheet and bake onion for 15 minutes, then flip and continue baking another 15 minutes, or until breading is brown. Meanwhile prepare sauce. Remove and place on a plate and salt immediately for taste.

FOR SAUCE:

8. Put all ingredients into a small bowl and whisk together until all ingredients are incorporated. Serve with the Rash and Bash Super Onion when it comes out of the oven.

HACK ATTACK!

SPINACH ATTACK

A lot of people don't make spinach because they don't want to clean it or steam it or hassle with it so if you fancy a cheese and spinach omelette or some spinach for a side dish or under your piece of foil cooked salmon (p.94) or to add to a "bowl" (p.128), just try this simple hack!

Take a bag of store-bought cleaned spinach, open the bag on one end and put in your microwave for about 2½ minutes on high. Carefully remove bag, it will be hot! Pour spinach on plate. You will have a perfectly steamed pile of spinach. You can squeeze out the liquid once it cools and chop up for creamed spinach.

If you don't want that gritty, weird feeling on your teeth when you eat spinach then do NOT add lemon juice or other citrus to raw or cooked spinach. Lemon zest works to brighten creamed spinach but that's up you, I personally avoid citrus with most spinach dishes because it makes my teeth hurt! :)

FAST CREAMED SPINACH

INGREDIENTS (serves 2):

1 bag washed spinach
1 small shallot or 2 Tbsp onion
2 Tbsp butter
Pinch cayenne pepper
Pinch ground nutmeg
¾ cup heavy cream
¼ cup grated Parmesan cheese

METHOD:

Squeeze all of the water out of the spinach then chop it up (you can use paper towels to remove the water). Mince the shallot or onion then saute in butter until shallot or onion is translucent, about 3-4 minutes. Add cayenne pepper, nutmeg, and cream, mix and cook for about 5 minutes on high until it is reduced a bit, stir often. Reduce heat and add spinach, stir then add cheese. Stir until cheese is well incorporated then serve immediately.

QUICK PEPPER SIDE

Peppers are incredibly healthy and tasty too, the capsicum in peppers is known to promote healthy endorphin release and they are chock full of Vitamin C. If you have the grill fired up then throw a bunch of these on and remember; about 10% of them will be VERY hot but the rest will be mild to eat :) You can also make these in a cast iron pan placed on a high heat on the stove top OR place the pan directly on the BBQ on high heat but be careful of the handle in both cases, very hot!

0:05 PREP TIME

0:10 COOK TIME

2-4 SERVINGS

INGREDIENTS

6–8 spicy peppers of your choice, I've been known to use Spanish Padron peppers or Japanese Shishito peppers

¼ cup oil depending on size of pan

METHOD

1. Place peppers in cast iron pan with a good layer of oil.

2. Cook until they are blistered all over. Remove and place on a serving plate.

3. Sprinkle with sea salt or soy sauce and serve.

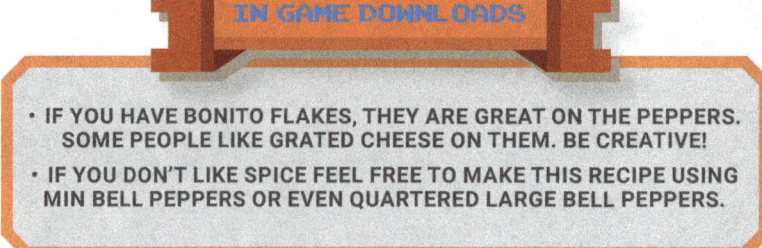

IN GAME DOWNLOADS

- IF YOU HAVE BONITO FLAKES, THEY ARE GREAT ON THE PEPPERS. SOME PEOPLE LIKE GRATED CHEESE ON THEM. BE CREATIVE!
- IF YOU DON'T LIKE SPICE FEEL FREE TO MAKE THIS RECIPE USING MIN BELL PEPPERS OR EVEN QUARTERED LARGE BELL PEPPERS.

AMAIZING ROASTED CORN

What happens when government scientists misinterpret a memo about corn, and genetically engineer sentient corn? You get the quirky game called Maize, in which the gamer (you) has to figure out strange puzzles while talking with strange objects. Sounds a lot like a Monty Python skit, doesn't it? But it also might make you hungry for some roasted corn – which is what you can make with the following recipe. If you're firing up the grill why not add a few ears of corn and make this fast, delicious Mexican-inspired treat? I love picking up an ear or two when I'm on Olvera street in Los Angeles, the street vendors have lovely charred, tasty examples of this yummy corn.

0:05 PREP TIME

0:05 COOK TIME

4 SERVINGS

Inspired by the video game Maize

INGREDIENTS

4 ears of corn, shucked
½ cup mayonnaise
¼ cup lime juice
1 tsp cayenne pepper
1 tsp chili powder
1 tsp salt
1 tsp pepper

METHOD

1. Grill the corn on all sides until the kernels are blackened to your taste.

2. Mix up mayonnaise, lime juice, chili powder or cayenne and salt and pepper to your taste in a small bowl and serve with the corn or slather it on and serve already dressed. Make sure you have napkins!!!

IN GAME DOWNLOADS

- IF YOU WANT IT THICKER, ADD LESS LIME JUICE
- IF YOU WANT TO BE MORE DECADENT PUT MELTED BUTTER ON THE CORN EARS FIRST THEN SLATHER ON THE SAUCE.
- IF YOU WANT TO BE HEALTHIER THEN SUBSTITUTE PLAIN YOGURT FOR THE MAYONNAISE.
- IF YOU WANT MORE SPICE ADD SOME OF YOUR FAVORITE HOT SAUCE.

Dressings & Sauces

"If you're in a hurry, using leftovers, or simply want to look like you've made some effort, try making a quick homemade dressing or sauce and elevate your dishes to the next level."

EPIC PERKY PESTO

In Epic Mickey, you take on the role of the iconic, perky mouse who is on a mission to bring a splash of color to the world that has lost nearly all its bright, brilliant colors. All he has to work with are his trusty paint brush and his brains that he uses to solve puzzles and splash colors all over the colorless world. Now you can also bring a splash of color to your foods, with this quick and versatile recipe and save your meals from being too flat on flavor or color. I always keep pesto on hand because it's so versatile and tasty! Pesto is a no brainer for your favorite pasta with a nice handful of fresh grated parmesan, can't be beat! But see the in game downloads for other ideas where to use Mickey's pesto. Be creative and enjoy :)

Inspired by the video game Epic Mickey

0:05 PREP TIME

0:00 COOK TIME

4-6 SERVINGS

INGREDIENTS

2 cups packed fresh basil leaves
2 cloves garlic
¼ cup pine nuts or walnuts (or half-half)
⅔ cup extra-virgin olive oil, divided
Kosher salt and freshly ground black pepper, to taste
½ cup freshly grated Pecorino cheese.

METHOD

1. Place the walnuts, pignolis, and garlic in the bowl of a food processor fitted with a steel blade. Process for 15 seconds.

2. Add the basil leaves, salt, and pepper.

3. With the processor running, slowly pour the olive oil into the bowl through the feed tube and process until the pesto is thoroughly pureed.

4. Add the cheese and puree for a minute. Use right away or store the pesto in the refrigerator or freezer with a thin film of olive oil on top.

IN GAME DOWNLOADS

- I FLATTEN CHICKEN BREASTS AND SMEAR THEM WITH PESTO, POP A SLICE OF CHEESE ON TOP AND ROLL THEM UP AND BROWN THEM ON THE STOVE, PUT A LITTLE CHICKEN STOCK IN THE PAN, PUT A LID ON AND VOILA, PERFECT ROLLED PESTO, CHEESY CHICKEN!
- I ALSO PUT PESTO ON SALMON BEFORE ROASTING IT WHEN I'M IN A HURRY.
- TRY A DOLLOP ON A CAPRESE SALAD (FRESH SLICED TOMATOES AND GOOD MOZZARELLA OR BURRATA CHEESE).
- PESTO IS EVEN GOOD IN WRAPS AND ON SCRAMBLED EGGS!

HACK ATTACK!

HACKS FOR PASTA

I usually have a nice homemade marinara in the fridge, which I use during the week for quick meals. I love a simple pasta of penne with marinara and some good burrata, mozzarella and or parmesan on top with maybe some fresh sautéed veggies thrown in. Whatever sauce or pesto you use on your pasta, why not try these hacks to give it a bit of extra zing!

HACK #1: You can add a little fresh lemon zest or a teaspoon of fresh lemon juice to the pasta for a bright note.

HACK #2: You can use penne or orrechiette pasta (little ear pasta) instead of farfalle.

HACK #3: You can add fresh or frozen peas.

HACK #4: You can add fresh minced chives instead of parsley to serve.

HACK #5: Add a little chopped scallion or sweet onion or a bit of cooked jalapeño for extra bite!

HACK #6: Make zucchini ribbons with a vegetable peeler and salt them so the water comes out. After 10 minutes squeeze the ribbons in your hands to remove all moisture, then use with some marinara sauce and cheese for a quick, healthy topping!

SUNDAY AFTERNOON SMASH TOMATO GRAVY

You've been playing Super Smash Brothers all day, and your fingers and arms are getting tired. You have out-dueled your gaming friends and now you're about to make you and your gaming friends something good to eat. Spaghetti and meatballs sounds good and this recipe for gravy will put your meal over the top and smash the competition! This recipe is based on one I saw Italian chef Marcella Hazen do on a cooking show ages ago. You can use this on Westballz Meatballs (p.65).

Inspired by the video game Super Smash Brothers

0:05 PREP TIME

0:45 COOK TIME

4 SERVINGS

INGREDIENTS

2 cans of whole tomatoes
1 stick of butter
1 medium onion
1 handful of basil or parsley
1 tsp Italian seasoning
Pinch of chili pepper flakes
¼ cup Parmesan cheese
Salt and pepper, to taste

METHOD

1. Put 2 cans of whole tomatoes in a big pot. Add a stick of butter.

2. Cut an onion in half horizontally and remove peel, place both halves, cut side down in pot with tomatoes and butter.

3. Cook, simmering for 45 minutes, squishing the tomatoes apart from time to time.

4. Take the onion out and throw it away. Season to taste with salt and pepper. Sauce is ready to use!

IN GAME DOWNLOADS

- TRY IT ON CHICKEN IN WRAPS.
- I ALSO USE THIS SAUCE FOR AN EASY CHICKEN PARMESAN MEAL: SIMPLY BAKE OR FRY FLATTENED, SEASONED, EGG-AND-PANKO-COATED CHICKEN BREASTS AND TOP WITH THIS SAUCE AND SOME CHEESE AND THROW UNDER A BROILER FOR A COUPLE OF MINUTES AND YOU HAVE A GREAT, FAST MEAL.
- THROW SOME FRESH BASIL AND OR RED CHILI PEPPER FLAKES ON TOP FOR EXTRA FLAVOR.
- YOU CAN ADD CHOPPED STEAMED, GRILLED OR SAUTÉED VEGETABLES TO THE SAUCE IF YOU WANT TO SNEAK SOME HEALTH INTO IT.

"THIS RECIPE IS BASED ON ONE I SAW ITALIAN CHEF MARCELLA HAZEN DO."

HACK ATTACK!

PERFECTLY COOKED FISH HACK

This is one of my favorite hacks. How to make sure you never make the common mistake of over-cooking your fish? Try this simple hack! Dress up your dinner by rubbing or marinating the fish before cooking. Or, 'just for the halibut', add a delicious simple sauce at the end (p.155).

HACK #1: Pre-heat oven to 400° then pop your fish in and turn the oven off. Leave for 10-20 minutes (depending on the thickness of the fish). When you come back, your fish is moist and delicious not dry and overcooked.

HACK #2: You can put shallots or garlic or onions in olive oil and rub over the fish before cooking. You can add any sort of spices you like such as Cajun or herbs de Provence for different flavors.

HACK #3: For an Asian flavor, try this marinade: mix soy sauce, sesame oil, chopped garlic, fresh ginger and a dash of lime juice. Pour over fish and leave for 20-30 minutes in fridge.

CC'S "JUST FOR THE HALIBUT" SAUCE

I love lots of wonderful healthy foods, and fish is at the top of that list. I'll grill it, poach it or roast it in the oven – using the hack I invented produces a perfectly-cooked piece of fish EVERY time! But I also have the perfect condiment to go along with a nicely cooked piece of fish. Try this out and you'll see why it's so awesome!

0:05 PREP TIME

0:00 COOK TIME

4-6 SERVINGS

INGREDIENTS

½ cup mayonnaise

½ cup sour cream

2 Tbsp Dijon mustard (or more to taste)

Juice of one small lemon

Fresh dill and parsley, chopped fine

One dill pickle, chopped fine

One green onion, chopped fine

Salt and pepper, to taste

METHOD

1. Mix all ingredients in small bowl and enjoy with pretty much any fish, even fish and chips!

Inspired by Claudia's devastating puns :)

IN GAME DOWNLOADS

- YOU CAN USE REGULAR WHITE OR RED ONION INSTEAD OF THE GREEN (SCALLION).
- YOU CAN USE DRIED HERBS IF YOU DO NOT HAVE FRESH.
- YOU CAN REDUCE THE LEMON TO HALF A LEMON IF YOU WANT A THICKER SAUCE.

ADDICTIVELY SWEET JALAPEÑO ROCKET RELISH

In the middle of a fast and furious round of Rocket League and need something sweet but with a kick, in order to get you revved-up for another round? Make some of this sweet and spicy jalapeño relish to have on-hand to put on top of nearly any type of dish. It's sweet, spicy and very pleasantly addictive! Goes especially well on a few High Octane Breakfast Hub Caps (p.105), or your favorite deli meat sandwich, or even on a nice juicy steak. Makes enough to fill several jars, so you'll have plenty to share if you want – or not! You will only need 1 to 2 tablespoons on whatever you make.

0:10 PREP TIME

0:15 COOK TIME

7 pt SERVINGS

INGREDIENTS

21 large jalapeño peppers*
8 cups sugar
2 Tbsp pickling spice
3 tsp salt
4 cups apple cider vinegar

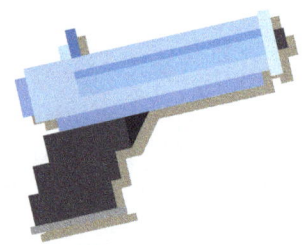

METHOD

1. **Wear rubber gloves!** Wash peppers, seed and either slice for pickles or chop/grind for relish. If making slices, soak in lime water overnight to make them crispy. The relish does not need to soak.

2. **Bring cider to a boil.** Add slices or relish and bring back to a boil.

3. **Keep at a low boil,** while filling clean, scalded jars. Seal with hot lids. Judge the amount of syrup by the number of peppers you have. If there is syrup left over, you can keep it in the fridge for other things like pickled beets or coleslaw.

(* Estimated based on the following formula given by my sister; number of peppers equal to 1 cucumber, multiplied by 7.)

Inspired by the video game Rocket League

IN GAME DOWNLOADS

• SERVE THIS RELISH ON VIRTUALLY ANYTHING YOU CAN THINK OF THAT IS SAVORY; STEAK, EGGS, TOAST – LET YOUR MIND RUN WILD! ONCE YOU EAT THIS, YOU'LL BE HOOKED!

FARMER'S BOUNTY HOT PEPPER RELISH

You have been playing Farmville for hours, and now you're getting hungry for something tasty. Wanna make some High Octane Breakfast Hub Caps (p.105) or some Hail to the King Hamburgers (p.108), but don't want to put the same old ketchup or mustard on it? Why not grab a jar of this hot pepper relish instead! It's spicy and sweet at the same time and uses fresh hot peppers. You can put it on virtually any savory dish you make for you and your gaming friends, and it compliments almost anything – even a juicy steak! This recipe makes enough for 7 pints of relish, but you'll only need a tablespoon to top off your meal.

Inspired by the video game Farmville

0:20 PREP TIME

0:35 COOK TIME

7 pt SERVINGS

INGREDIENTS

18 green peppers
18 red chili peppers, stemmed (you can use green peppers for a milder flavor)
6–8 onions, peeled
1 Tbsp canning salt
2½ cups cider vinegar
1¾ cups sugar

METHOD

1. Chop up peppers and onions; make it easy on yourself by using a food processor to chop the vegetables! Place in 6-quart pot. Add salt and cover with boiling water. Let stand for 10 minutes.

2. Drain water, then add vinegar and sugar, bring to a boil, then let simmer for 20 minutes. Spoon into 7 pint-sized jars, pressing down as you spoon to allow liquid to cover the vegetables in the jars.

3. At this point the pepper relish is ready for immediate use – just wipe rims off and put the lids on. But if you're not going to use all of the relish quickly, you can always use a traditional canning process to allow you to store the relish in jars for months!

CANNING METHOD:

4. Wipe the rims of all the jars clean, and place canning lids on jars.

5. Move the jars into a processing pot of water and bring to a boil. When water begins to boil, start timer for 15 minutes to ensure jars are properly sealed and sterile.

6. Once jars have boiled in water for 15 minutes, remove and allow to cool – use canning tongs or heat-resistant gloves to remove the jars from the boiling water.

7. After jars have cooled, tap the tops of the jars, if any of the lids pops up, simply place into the fridge and use relatively soon. The jars that have been properly sealed can be stored at room temperature for several months!

WAR GOD SALAD DRESSING

The gods of Olympus have given Cretos a new lease on life; having been betrayed by mortals, he has returned to repay their heinous act with cold hard vengeance – and awesome weaponry like his double chain axes. But even the god of war needs to take a time out to have some good grub, and Cretos enjoys a nice meal, including a salad with his God of War Salad Dressing on it! Makes 8 ounces of dressing.

- 0:05 PREP TIME
- 0:00 COOK TIME
- 1-2 SERVINGS

INGREDIENTS

3 cloves garlic
½ tsp salt
⅓ cup Parmesan cheese
2 Tbsp Dijon mustard
1 tsp Worcestershire sauce
1 tsp sugar
⅓ cup fresh squeezed lemon juice
1 cup olive oil
2 Tbsp fresh parsley

METHOD

1. Place all ingredients into blender except olive oil, then begin to blend.

2. Slowly stream in olive oil into mixture until blended completely. Drizzle on your salad and enjoy!

Inspired by the video game God of War

SLIME DRESSING

You've been playing slime rancher all day on your Xbox One, attempting to not only catch new slime breeds, but find enough food to feed those in your slime pens at the ranch. It's late and you're now hungry after a long day out in the field. why not make a batch of Slime Dressing to go with an order of your favorite vegetable or an order of Crashbreaker Chips (p.212)? Put your feet up, check your intergalactic messages and enjoy a late-night snack on the ranch.

Inspired by the video game Slime Rancher

0:05 PREP TIME

0:00 COOK TIME

2 SERVINGS

INGREDIENTS

2 Tbsp fresh parsley *
1 Tbsp chopped dill
2 Tbsp chopped chives
2 tsp salt
2 tsp pepper
½ cup sour cream
1 cup mayonnaise
½–1 cup buttermilk
1 tsp white vinegar
(*instead of parsley, you can substitute Italian seasoning mix)

METHOD

1. Chop parsley, dill and chives.

2. Put sour cream, mayonnaise, salt, pepper and buttermilk, and vinegar into blender, along with the herbs.

3. Blend until creamy and smooth. Pour into dip cup and enjoy with veggies or Crashbreaker Chips (recipe p.212).

IN GAME DOWNLOADS

- IF YOU DON'T HAVE BUTTERMILK ON HAND, SEE THE SIMPLE HACK ON P.69 FOR HOW TO MAKE SOME!
- ALSO, WHEN MAKING THE RANCH DRESSING, TRY ADDING A FEW DASHES OF YOUR FAVORITE HOT SAUCE IN BEFORE BLENDING. YOU CAN ALSO ADD CHIPOTLE PEPPER POWDER TO ACHIEVE A SIMILAR KICK TO THE DRESSING/DIP!

Desserts & Sweets

"You can hack your way to a sweet finish for any meal with these delicious recipes."

MAD BOMBER APPLE PIE POPPERS

The Mad Bomber is at it again; only instead of explosive bombs, he's co-opted the kitchen to make amazing little apple bombs. These little packets of sweet goodness are sure to go boom in your mouth with an explosion of flavor! You can make as few or as many as you'd like, but just be sure not to drop any, because there isn't a safety net below to catch them. This recipe can make as many as 4 or up to 20, depending on the size of your gaming party.

Inspired by the video game Kaboom!

0:10 PREP TIME

0:15 COOK TIME

4-20 SERVINGS

INGREDIENTS

2 apples peeled and diced finely
2 Tbsp brown sugar
1½ Tbsp cinnamon
1 Tbsp melted butter
4 (or more) wonton wrappers
Water – to seal wontons
Powdered sugar for serving

METHOD

1. Pre-heat oven to 350°. Place diced apples, brown sugar, cinnamon and melted butter into a large bowl and mix thoroughly so that all apple pieces are coated.

2. Take 1 wonton wrapper and spoon out ¼ teaspoon of apple mixture into center of wrapper. Wet your fingers with water and moisten the sides of the wonton wrappers, then place 2nd wonton wrapper on top. Press firmly to seal. (Alternative method: place wonton in position so it forms a diamond, put ¼ teaspoon of apple mixture in center, then moisten the edges of wrapper and fold over and seal so wrapper forms a triangle.)

3. Repeat for remaining wontons, until apple mixture is gone.

4. Place wontons onto sprayed baking sheet and bake for 15 minutes, flipping apple wontons halfway through.

5. Remove from oven and dust with powdered sugar and serve.

IN GAME DOWNLOADS

- INSTEAD OF BAKING THE PIES ON A BAKING SHEET, TRY THE FOLLOWING METHOD: SPRAY A CUPCAKE PAN WELL WITH COOKING SPRAY, THEN GENTLY PUT A WONTON WRAPPER INTO EACH CUP, THEN PLACE 1 TEASPOON OF APPLE FILLING IN THE MIDDLE AND BAKE AT 350° FOR 15 MINUTES. YOU'LL GET APPLE-FILLED CUPS THAT ARE JUST AS TASTY AND DELICIOUS AS THE SHEET-BAKED VARIETY.
- FOR EXTRA BONUS ACHIEVEMENT POINTS, TRY MAKING YOUR OWN POWDERED SUGAR (SEE HACK ON P.183)

ROMANCING THE HACK WITH KATHLEEN TURNER & MARTIN LANDAU

KATHLEEN TURNER

OKAY, so imagine a time when there are no cell phones and no instant food delivery and no online shopping. I know, it's difficult, but just stay with me. I get a call on my land line from a friend from New York City who tells me he's just landed at LAX with two very well-known actors: Kathleen Turner, star of Romancing the Stone with Michael Douglas and more recently on Californication with David Duchovney; and Martin Landau, who has been in everything but notably Alfred Hitchcock's North by Northwest—most definitely worth a watch if you haven't seen it, and if you have worth a rewatch— and more recently as a guest star on Entourage.

"They don't want to deal with a restaurant or being stared at and they're starving. Can they come over to eat?" my friend asked. "Sure, no problemo, swing on by," I reply. As I hang up I remember that my car is in the shop and it's raining so taking my motorcycle out for groceries is not an option. Shit. LA roads are treacherous when it rains because of the layer of oil that rises to the top—a slippery death for bikers. Time to get my hack on.

First, survey the fridge. There were some decent greens so I knew I could make a salad but it was raining so I needed something comforting. There's a rack of lamb in the freezer so I stick it in the microwave on defrost and start rummaging through the pantry. LAX is 45 minutes from my house, the rain might buy me a little extra time, but I was in full hustle mode.

Yank some faro from the pantry and stick it in salted water. Set the table. While the faro cooks I pull the defrosted lamb out of the microwave and make a quick marinade of soy sauce, Dijon mustard, olive oil, honey, rosemary, thyme and garlic. I season the rack then smear the marinade on and set it aside. Quickly roast some walnuts in a pan and then in a big bowl I put the juice of three lemons, a third of a cup of olive oil, some minced scallions, a cup of golden raisins and a whole can of green olives that I roughly chop.

I drain the faro and add it to the ingredients in the bowl, give it a good stir and season it then I add the chopped walnuts and some chopped parsley and parmesan cheese, it's delicious. I put that aside as it will be perfect at room temperature with extra shavings of Parmesan on it before serving. I whip up a nice simple salad dressing with Dijon, balsamic vinegar, a little minced garlic and olive oil, season that and set aside.

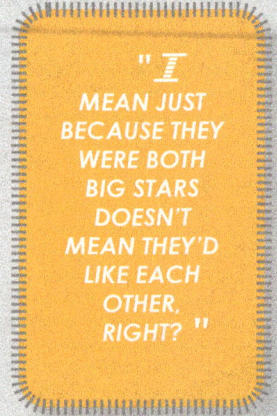

"*I* MEAN JUST BECAUSE THEY WERE BOTH BIG STARS DOESN'T MEAN THEY'D LIKE EACH OTHER, RIGHT?"

Dessert! I know I have good vanilla ice cream so I make a quick caramel sauce with sugar, cream, butter and salt then set that aside. I'll serve the ice cream in a martini glass with the caramel sauce and a butter cookie sticking out of it, okay not exactly a soufflé but it looks cute and tastes wonderful. Of course I wish I had some puff pastry in the freezer and a few apples because then I would have whipped up a nice warm tart but I'm doing the best I can.

I clean the greens and shave some celery, fennel and carrot into the salad and cover the bowl with a wet paper towel. I light the fire and open a bottle of red wine and put a bottle of fizzy water on the table, whew! Time is going quickly but I know when they get here I'll be totally fine. I put some nuts out in a bowl, change my clothes and put on a little makeup and I'm good to go.

My guests arrive, and the lamb is in the oven, I threw some sliced carrots in the pan to roast with the lamb as well, so they will be nicely caramelized. We chat and they have a glass of wine in front of the fire. I take the lamb out to rest, put the two salads on the table and then cut the rack of lamb and place on a serving dish with the roast carrots around it, sprinkle a little chopped parsley on top and dinner is served.

I was a bit hesitant about the small group. I mean just because they were both big stars doesn't mean they'd like each other, right? Plus they both had rather large personalities, so would it be a bust? My worries were for naught, the night was hilarious, we all had fun and got on well and the meal was a big success. I suppose a few bottles of wine didn't hurt the mood either. Here were some of my impression at the time:

I was so happy that neither one of them were vegetarians, they loved every bit of the lamb and wiped their plates clean.

Kathleen Turner has always been really fascinating to me, she seemed to live her life the way she wanted to, spirited and independent and tough. She turned down roles when she thought the scripts were weak, fought for equal pay before it was trendy and also battled with a grave illness, rheumatoid arthritis. She lived up to my expectations and was a hilarious, vibrant dinner guest who got on well with Martin and complimented me numerous times on my home and my cooking. A real dame!

The conversation at the table was lively, ranging from the topic of the times—the beating of Rodney King and the subsequent riots in Los Angeles—to plays they'd both love to do, to characters they wish they would have been cast in.

Once they were gone I was proud of myself for pulling a rabbit out of the hat and turning on a great impromptu meal. Most importantly I learned the importance of having a protein in the freezer and some vegetables on hand if you have to entertain on the spot.

SHARING ANOTHER MEAL WITH MARTIN LANDAU IN PALERMO, SICILY.

TURNER AND LANDAU CARAMEL SAUCE

This is the recipe I made when I had two famous unexpected guests show up on a rainy evening in La La Land, the lickety-split sauce made simple ice cream and a cookie into an elegant dessert! This recipe serves 6 easily with a nice portion of sauce to keep in an airtight container for future sweet evenings.

0:02 PREP TIME

0:05 COOK TIME

6 SERVINGS

INGREDIENTS

1 cup sugar (I use dark brown for caramel)
½ cup heavy whipping cream
⅓ stick of butter
Pinch of sea salt
1 tsp vanilla extract

METHOD

1. In a medium saucepan, mix together the sugar, heavy whipping cream, butter and salt and bring to a boil. Reduce the heat to medium-low and let the mixture simmer for about 2 minutes, whisking occasionally.

2. Remove the saucepan from the heat, add the vanilla extract (be careful, the mixture is hot) and stir. Let mixture cool in the pan for 2 minutes, then pour into a jar.

3. Let cool to room temperature and refrigerate until ready to use (up to 5 days). Warm it up in the microwave before using.

IN GAME DOWNLOADS

- TO MAKE A SALTED CARAMEL SAUCE EITHER ADD MORE SALT (⅓ TEASPOON) TO THE SAUCE WHILE COOKING OR BETTER YET, SPRINKLE CRUNCHY SEA SALT OVER THE DESSERT BEFORE SERVING.

"Dessert! I know I have good vanilla ice cream so I make a quick caramel sauce with sugar, cream butter and salt then set that aside."

IN GAME DOWNLOADS

- ADD FRESH BERRIES, HOMEMADE CARAMEL OR CHOCOLATE SAUCES, SOME CRUMBLED AMARETTO COOKIES AND A DOLLOP OF FRESH WHIPPED CREAM... USE YOUR CREATIVITY, THE SKY'S THE LIMIT!

DANCING PENGUIN EASY VANILLA ICE CREAM

In Happy Feet the game, you take on the lead role from the movie of the same name. You may find yourself either trying to keep time with your dance moves, sliding across the ice to gather fish while beating the clock, or just dropping a fishing line in order to grab some fish, but either way, you will have a fun time, and work up a bit of an appetite. If you want a cool and fun treat, try making some of this easy vanilla ice cream. Vanilla ice cream is a wonderful base for a quick creative dessert, however, the ice cream must be of good quality and how better to know what's in it then to whip it up yourself? Here's an ice cream base that will allow you to make a batch of ice cream in almost no time at all, and cause you to have happy feet as your taste buds dance for joy!

4:10 PREP TIME

0:05 COOK TIME

8-10 SERVINGS

Inspired by the video game Happy Feet

INGREDIENTS

- 2 cups heavy cream, preferably not ultra-pasteurized
- 2 cups half-and-half (or 1 cup additional heavy cream plus 1 cup whole milk)
- 1–2 tsp vanilla extract
- 1 cup granulated sugar or ¾ cup light corn syrup, more to taste
- ½ tsp salt

METHOD

1. In a saucepan or a microwave-safe container, combine cream, half-and-half, and vanilla. On the stove or in the microwave, bring mixture to a simmer. Immediately turn off heat or remove from microwave.

2. Add sugar or corn syrup and salt and mix until sugar dissolves, about 1 minute. Taste and add more sugar and salt as needed to balance the flavors. The mixture should taste slightly too sweet before freezing it, it'll calm down after it's frozen.

3. Pour mixture into a container (I use a glass loaf pan) and refrigerate until very cold, at least 4 hours and preferably overnight.

4. Churn mixture in an ice cream maker according to manufacturer's instructions. Serve immediately or transfer to an airtight container and let freeze until hard.

HACK ATTACK!

NO MACHINE ICE CREAM

Want to try making ice cream without a machine? Here's a simple hack.

Prepare your ice cream mixture (see p.171 for a great recipe idea), then chill it over an ice bath.

Put a deep baking dish, or bowl made of plastic, stainless steel or something durable in the freezer, and pour your ice cream mixture into it.

After forty-five minutes, open the door and check it. As it starts to freeze near the edges, remove it from the freezer and stir it vigorously with a spatula or whisk. Really beat it up and break up any frozen sections. Return to freezer.

Continue to check the mixture every 30 minutes, stirring vigorously as it's freezing. If you have one, you can use a hand-held mixer or stick blender for best results.

Keep checking periodically and stirring while it freezes (by hand or with the electric mixer) until the ice cream is frozen. It will likely take 2-3 hours to be ready.

OPTIONAL HACKS: When the ice cream is slightly frozen add your "hacks": chocolate bits, candy, swirls of peanut or almond butter, caramel, fruit jams, fresh fruit, spices... use your imagination!

BANANA HOARD ICE CREAM

Donkey Kong and Diddy Kong have finally taken back Donkey Kong's hoard of bananas that K. Rool stole. To celebrate, Donkey Kong, Diddy, and the rest of the Kong family are having a celebration. What are they going to be serving for dessert? Banana Hoard Ice Cream, of course. Named after Donkey Kong himself, this wonderful frozen treat is a snap to make, and only needs one main ingredient; bananas! But you can go ape by adding in chocolate syrup, cinnamon or even nuts. This wonderful dessert will feed up to 12 of your banana-crazed gamer friends.

Inspired by the video game Donkey Kong Country

3:05 PREP TIME

0:00 COOK TIME

12 SERVINGS

INGREDIENTS

4 ripe bananas

METHOD

1. Peel and cut bananas into chunks.

2. Freeze in a plastic container or re-sealable bag for two to three hours.

3. Remove and place in blender and blend until smooth. Scoop and enjoy!

IN GAME DOWNLOADS

- WHILE BLENDING THE MIXTURE, YOU CAN ADD IN ANY TYPE OF NUT OR DRIED FRUIT—EVEN CINNAMON AND CHOCOLATE SAUCE CAN BE ADDED TO GIVE THE ICE CREAM YOUR OWN "KRAZY KOMBINATION".
- DONKEY KONG HAS BEEN KNOWN TO LOVE HIS BANANA ICE CREAM PLAIN, BUT DIDDY KONG IS RUMORED TO ENJOY CHOCOLATE IN HIS! TRY DIFFERENT FLAVORS AND COMBINATIONS TO MAKE THIS YOUR OWN… JUST BE SURE TO LEAVE SOME BANANAS FOR OL' DONKEY KONG TO ENJOY!

PACNANA ICE CREAM PIE

Good old Pac-Man has been around since nearly the start of video gaming and chomping on pac-pellets since 1980. You know he has to be getting pretty tired of eating the same thing all the time, so why not make him a Pacnana Ice Cream Pie to satisfy ol' Pac's sweet tooth wedge mouth, or whatever it is Pac-Man eats with!

Inspired by the video game Pac-Man

6:05 PREP TIME

0:15 COOK TIME

12 SERVINGS

INGREDIENTS

FOR THE CRUST:
6 Tbsp butter, melted
1½ cups finely ground graham cracker crumbs
⅓ cup white sugar

FOR THE FILLING:
4 bananas
16 oz heavy whipping cream
8 oz whipped cream (optional)

METHOD

MAKE THE CRUST:
1. In a food processor, grind graham crackers pretty fine, but not to dust. Mix in sugar then drizzle in melted butter until all graham crackers are coated.

2. Pour cracker crumbs into pre-buttered (or sprayed) pie pan and press, ensuring crumb crust comes up the sides of pan.

3. Preheat oven to 350°. Bake crust between 12 and 15 minutes until crust is firm. Remove from oven and place pan on a wire rack to completely cool.

ADD THE FILLING:
4. Mash up ripe bananas and place into a blender along with the heavy cream. Blend until completely smooth, then pour into cooled pie crust.

5. Place in freezer for at least 2 hours for a slightly frozen pie, and up to 6 hours to completely firm up. Slice piece and enjoy with whipped cream, plain, or with your favorite topping.

HACK ATTACK!

FAKING FANCY PUFF PASTRY 2.0

Do yourself a favor and buy a couple of boxes of puff pastry dough and leave it in your freezer, it will come in handy some day I promise. Some of my favorite sweet and savory snacks and starters have come from that little box in the freezer. How about a quick dessert? Check out this great hack, and don't forget the savory ones (p.23)!

SUPER FAST PASTRY DESSERT

INGREDIENTS:

1 sheet puff pastry
1 egg, beaten
Finishing or turbinado sugar

TOPPINGS:
Try any of the following combinations:

Nutella and chopped almonds
Peanut butter and jelly
Jam and cream cheese
Honey and spices
Apple butter and cinnamon
Or experiment with your own!

METHOD:

Place the thawed puff pastry sheet on a piece of parchment paper and smear over it your choice of toppings. Leave about 2" around the perimeter of the sheet with no filling on it.
Make sure the spreads are room temperature or warm so they spread more easily and don't break the pastry dough.
Then role the sheet up tightly, slice down the middle and then braid those two pieces together. Brush on egg wash (beaten egg) and sprinkle with sugar. Bake on a parchment-lined baking sheet at 350° for about 20 minutes until it's nice and golden and puffed up. You will have a huge braid which you can share with everyone or eat yourself!

CLAUDIA'S DEADLY DISC SUMMER CITRUS PIE

Playing Tron Deadly Discs on your Mattel Intellivision system is serious old-school fun. Run around and fight in the same computer world that my Babylon 5 co-star Bruce Boxleitner helped to liberate in the original 80s movie. You've been fighting all day and now you need to recharge your power source and disc, and what sweeter way to do it than with a slice of this summer citrus pie. You can make it ahead of time and have it on-hand when you and your other inhabitants of the Tron world need to take out the bad programs.

Inspired by the video game Tron Deadly Disks

4:10 PREP TIME

0:25 COOK TIME

8 SERVINGS

INGREDIENTS

FOR THE CRUST:
- 1½ cups ground graham crackers
- ⅓ cup white or brown sugar
- 6 Tbsp melted butter
- ½ tsp ground cinnamon
- OR, 1 ready-made graham cracker crust

FOR THE FILLING:
- 4 egg yolks
- 1 can (14 oz) sweetened condensed milk
- ½ cup lemon or lime juice, or a mix of the two
- Pinch of kosher salt
- Fresh whipped cream, lemon or lime zest, and flaky sea salt for garnish

METHOD

MAKE THE CRUST (If using ready-made crust, skip to step 4):

1. Heat oven to 375°. Using a food processor or your hands, pulse or crush the crackers finely (stop before all the crackers turn to dust; it's okay if you have some little pieces).

2. Add sugar and cinnamon, then butter. Pulse to combine or work the butter in with your hands until the crumbs hold together like dough.

3. Press into and up the sides of a 9-inch pie pan. Bake for 5–7 minutes then let cool completely.

ADD THE FILLING:

4. While the crust is cooling, in a medium bowl, whisk egg yolks into condensed milk, then whisk in the lemon or lime juice (or both) and salt, making sure to combine them completely.

5. Pour into the shell and bake for 14–16 minutes until the filling has set. Refrigerate until completely cold, 4 hours up to overnight.

6. Cover pie with thick waves of fresh whipped cream, grate the lemon or lime zest right over the whipped cream and add a little sprinkling of flaky sea salt, if desired. I do not sweeten the whipped cream because the pie is sweet enough but sometimes I add a half a teaspoon of vanilla extract to the cream before whipping. Both work nicely!

HOT TOP MOLTEN CHOCOLATE CAKE

Diddy Kong and his friends are racing to the top of Hot Top Volcano in order to see who is the best kart racer in Kong Land. But there won't be a sparkly trophy for the winner at the top, there will be yummy molten chocolate cakes. Diddy Kong has even sent us the recipe for this amazing snack.

0:10 PREP TIME

0:16 COOK TIME

4 SERVINGS

Inspired by the video game Diddy Kong Racing

INGREDIENTS

- 1 stick unsalted butter, plus melted butter for brushing
- 1 Tbsp unsweetened cocoa powder
- 1 tsp espresso powder or instant coffee (optional but enhances the chocolate flavor)
- ¼ cup plus 1 Tbsp all-purpose flour
- 6 oz dark chocolate (70% cacao), chopped (I use bars, not chips)
- ½ cup granulated sugar
- 3 large eggs, at room temperature
- Pinch of salt
- 4 heaped tsp cold, store-bought caramel sauce
- Flaky Maldon sea salt for sprinkling
- Confectioners' sugar for sprinkling

METHOD

1. Preheat the oven to 425°. Brush four 6-oz ramekins with melted butter. In a small bowl, whisk the cocoa powder with 1 tablespoon of the flour; dust the ramekins with the cocoa mixture, tapping out the excess. Transfer the ramekins to a sturdy baking sheet or pan.

2. In a medium saucepan, melt 1 stick of butter with the chocolate over very low heat, stirring occasionally. Let cool slightly.

3. In a bowl, using an electric mixer, beat the granulated sugar with the eggs and salt at medium-high speed until thick and pale yellow, 3 minutes.

4. Using a rubber spatula, fold in the melted chocolate until no streaks remain. Fold in the ¼ cup of flour and the espresso powder or instant coffee if using.

5. Spoon two-thirds of the batter into the prepared ramekins, then spoon 1 heaping teaspoon of caramel into each ramekin. Sprinkle with sea salt and cover with the remaining chocolate batter.

"Beat the granulated sugar with the eggs and salt at medium-high speed until thick and pale yellow."

6. Bake in the center of the oven for 16 minutes, until the tops are cracked but the centers are still slightly jiggly.

7. Transfer the ramekins to a rack and let cool for 5 to 8 minutes. Run the tip of a small knife around each cake to loosen. Invert a small plate over each cake and, using pot holders, invert again. Carefully lift off the ramekins.

8. Dust the warm cakes with confectioners' sugar and serve immediately. Serve with whipped cream or vanilla ice cream.

BULLET COMBO CHOCOLATE BROWNIES

While you're hunting down Soranno and trying to keep Ishi from succumbing to his newly-acquired cybernetic implants, you'll need quick energy to create some crazy bullet storm combos. Make a batch of these brownie muffins, and you'll even turn Soranno into a happy camper. Everyone needs a little chocolate!

0:10 PREP TIME

0:23 COOK TIME

20 SERVINGS

INGREDIENTS

3 cups bran cereal
2½–3 cups water
1 box (18¼ oz) fudge brownie mix
1 cup chocolate chips
1½ tsp baking powder

METHOD

1. Preheat the oven to 350°. Prepare muffin tin or brownie pan with cooking spray. Soak the cereal with water until all absorbed.

2. Mix the baking powder with the dry brownie mix, then add to the cereal mixture until well blended. I use a hand mixer.

3. Mix in chocolate chips by hand with a spatula.

4. Scoop batter into muffin cups or into pan.

5. Bake for approximately 23 minutes, until a toothpick can be inserted and removed cleanly without batter on it. Allow to cool before removing from muffin tin or cutting into 2-inch squares.

Inspired by the video game Bullet Storm

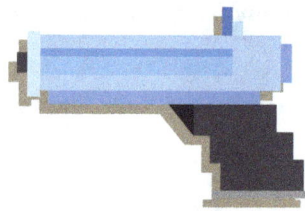

HACK ATTACK!

POWDERED SUGAR

Only have regular white granulated sugar in the cupboard? For extra bonus achievement points, try making your own powdered sugar. This is also known as confectioners' sugar.

HACK #1: Simply place 2 cups of granulated sugar and 2 teaspoons of cornstarch into a blender or food processor and blend until the sugar is a powdery consistency.

HACK #2: If you want really fine salt or sugar, just turn it into a fine dust by sticking it in a clean coffee grinder and grinding it up for a few seconds, it will stick to each kernel! This is great for popcorn (p.198)!

ANTI-DALEK KETO BROWNIES

What gamer hasn't wanted to take on the role of the time-traveling Doctor from Doctor Who? In Dalek Attack for the PC, you – the gamer – get that chance! You can play as my personal favorite Doctor (the 4th) and battle against one of his arch nemeses the Daleks as they try to exterminate all humanity from existence. As you play Dalek Attack, you can also attack your hunger with these sugar-free, gluten-free and Keto-friendly brownies which are a healthy treat you can enjoy while you "eradicate" your snack urge!

Patricia Tallman and I have traveled together many times but the last time a new, more serious situation arose; Pat found out that she is diabetic. I love to cook for us when we travel so I tailored our meal plans to avoid carbs and sugar and we happily noshed our way through the South West of France. Upon our return I had a dinner party for the ladies of B5 and Pat brought these delicious brownies for dessert, finally something sweet she could safely eat!

0:10 PREP TIME

0:15 COOK TIME

16 SERVINGS

Inspired by the video game Dalek Attack for the PC

INGREDIENTS

9 Tbsp butter
1 cup powdered erythritol, xylitol, or coconut sugar, if Paleo (Do NOT use stevia!)
½ cup + 3 Tbsp cocoa powder
½ tsp salt
2 eggs at room temperature
¾ cup almond flour
Flakey sea salt, for garnish (optional)

METHOD

1. Pre heat oven 350°. Line 8x8-inch baking pan with butter and parchment paper on bottom.

2. Add butter, Swerve and cocoa powder and salt to a medium heatproof bowl. Melt over a water bath, whisking constantly. Remove from bath. Let cool slightly.

3. Add one egg at a time. Whisk well. Add almond flour.

4. Bake for 15 minutes and check to make sure it isn't scorching. Check every few minutes til done. It will be fudgy and sticky.

5. Sprinkle with flakey salt if desired. Let cool as long as you can before cutting. It's hard because they smell amazing!

MARK'S LATE NIGHT DUNGEON CRAWLING

WHEN I was a freshman in High School, my best friend, John introduced me to a computer game that he loved playing. When we weren't playing pickup sports outside, building plastic models, playing Monopoly or games on his family's Atari 2600, we spent a lot of time in his mother's home office playing the game Wizardry on her Apple II computer.

> "WIZARDRY WAS ONE OF THE FIRST COMPUTER GAME TO GIVE USERS A FIRST-PERSON PERSPECTIVE."

Released in 1985 and written by two Cornell University students, Wizardry was more or less a computerized version Dungeons & Dragons. The difference between Wizardry and D&D was that Wizardry was the first computer game to give users a first-person perspective while making their way through the game.

We would grab a rather large stash of snacking goodies – cookies, chips, sodas and other required gamer fuel, so we could spend the whole night venturing into the dungeon. We had plenty of graphing paper, so we could map out the mazes we were traversing on our quest to defeat the mad wizard Werdna!

John and I would spend countless hours making our way through the dungeons in Wizardry and finding amazing weapons to battle the monsters within the game. At one point, we discovered a secret (after many hours of frustrating game play) that allowed us to create an incredibly powerful team member for our 6-member crew. Then we discovered how to duplicate that character enough to fill all 6 slots in our dungeon party. From then on, we were able to waltz through the game.

We would spend hours at that green-colored monitor, trying to beat the game, only to eventually succumb to our need for sleep. But we would always vow to continue the game the next day until his parents told us to go outside and play.

I still remember all the names of my Wizardry characters, and what type of character they were – even after all these years.

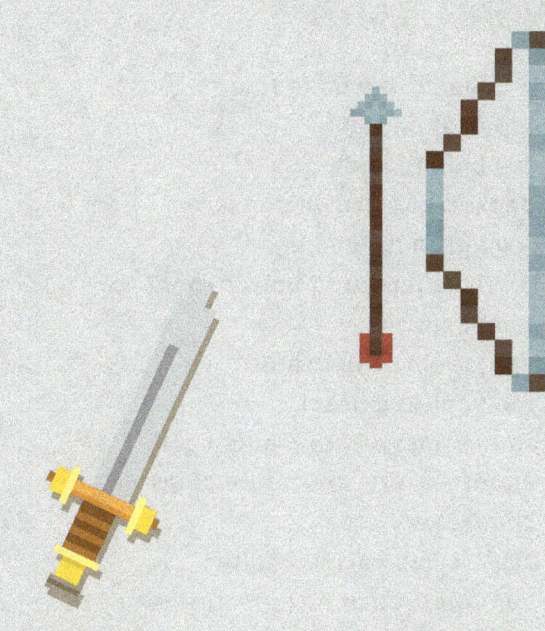

BADASS COOKIES!

Tiny Tina has gathered Brick, Mordecai, and the rest of her Pandoran friends together for their weekly round of Boderlands 2: Bunkers & Badasses! No, not the computer game, this time I'm talking about an actualy tabletop game. The gang is all set around the table, the 20-sided dice are at the ready and even Mr. Torgue is here to add in some of his trade-mark high-testosterone-laced comments! The only thing missing is Tiny Tina's favorite thing of all – cookies! Why not help her out and make a batch of her signature cookies, which have just about everything but skag teeth in them! This recipe makes about 20 cookies.

Inspired by the video game Borderlands 2

0:15 PREP TIME

0:17 COOK TIME

20 SERVINGS

INGREDIENTS

2¼ cups all-purpose flour

1 tsp kosher salt

1 tsp baking soda

1 packed cup brown sugar

½ cup granulated sugar

1½ sticks unsalted butter room temperature

1 egg, room temperature

1 tsp vanilla extract

About ¾ cup sweet treats such as toffee bits, chocolate chips or chunks, etc.

About ¾ cup various salty yummies, such as nuts, broken mini pretzels, corn chips or potato chips, etc

METHOD

1. In a bowl, whisk flour, salt and baking soda together. In a stand mixer, cream butter and sugars together at medium speed for about 2 minutes.

2. Mix in egg and vanilla. In three batches, add the dry ingredients, making sure previous batch is fully incorporated into mixture.

3. In a bowl, combine the sweet and salty mix-ins. Fold treat mixings by hand to the batter until evenly distributed.

4. Roll dough into a log about 2 inches in diameter, wrap and chill at least 1 hour or up to 2 days.

5. Heat oven to 325°. Line two cookie sheets with parchment paper or nonstick baking mats. Slice the dough into approximately ½-inch-thick disks and arrange on cookie sheets leaving 2 inches between cookies.

6. Bake until golden, about 20 minutes, rotating the pans halfway through. When done, the edges should be just brown and the tops should feel soft. Let cool on the pans for 5 minutes, then transfer to wire racks to finish cooling.

CLAUDIA'S FAIRY GODMOTHER COOKIES

I was cast to play the Fairy Godmother in the Shrek Forever After video game, voice matching Jennifer Saunders, the actress from Absolutely Fabulous, who plays the part in the movie. It's one of my favourite British comedy shows so I was chuffed to get the part. So here are come cookies inspired by my experience. They're so yummy you'll be asking your fairy godmother for more! Makes about 24 cookies.

Inspired by the video game Shrek Forever

0:15 PREP TIME

0:17 COOK TIME

24 SERVINGS

INGREDIENTS

3 cups all-purpose flour
1 Tbsp baking soda
1 Tbsp ground cinnamon
1 tsp salt
1 Tbsp baking powder
1½ cups (3 sticks) butter, at room temperature
1½ cups granulated sugar
3 eggs
1 Tbsp vanilla
1½ cups packed light-brown sugar
3 cups semisweet chocolate chips
3 cups old-fashioned rolled oats
2 cups (8 oz) chopped pecans
2 cups unsweetened flake coconut

METHOD

1. Pre-heat oven to 350°. Mix flour, cinnamon, salt, baking powder and baking soda in a separate bowl.

2. In a large mixing bowl, mix butter until smooth consistency. Add sugars slowly until incorporated nicely. Add eggs, one at a time into mixture, allowing them to get completely mixed in before adding the next one. Add vanilla.

3. Mix in flour mixture until just combined, then stir in chips, coconut, oats and pecans.

4. Drop about ⅛ cup or a large tablespoon of dough mixture onto cookie sheet (ungreased), leaving 3 inches between each cookie to allow them to spread out while baking. Bake at 350° for 15 to 17 minutes - turning baking sheet halfway through the baking.

5. Remove cookies from sheet and place on wire rack to cool completely. Store cookies in an air-tight container.

IN GAME DOWNLOADS

- TRY ADDING OTHER TYPES OF NUTS OR CHIPS AND EVEN DRIED FRUIT TO BATTER BEFORE BAKING. MIX IT UP AND FIND OUT WHAT SPROUTS UP!

- IF YOU DON'T HAVE A STAND MIXER, YOU CAN ALSO USE A FOOD PROCESSOR! PLACE NUTS IN FOOD PROCESSOR AND CHOP FAIRLY FINELY THEN POUR INTO SEPARATE BOWL. PUT BUTTER, SUGARS, EGGS, AND VANILLA INTO FOOD PROCESSOR AND MIX UNTIL SMOOTH. ADD DRY INGREDIENTS (FLOUR, BAKING SODA, CINNAMON, SALT, BAKING POWDER, OATS AND COCONUT) AND PROCESS UNTIL DRY INGREDIENTS ARE JUST INCORPORATED. DUMP MIXTURE INTO A LARGER MIXING BOWL AND POUR IN THE CHOCOLATE CHIPS AND NUTS. FOLD CHOCOLATE AND NUTS INTO MIXTURE USING A SPATULA OR SPOON UNTIL INCORPORATED, THEN PROCEED WITH THE BAKING PROCESS FROM STEP 4 OF METHOD.

HACK ATTACK!

DESSERT HACK: ETON MESS

When you play Strawberry Shortcake on the Atari 2600, your job is to match up the various characters from Shortcake's world to fun music. There are many different matchups since there are many different characters. But why stop the matching there? You can also try matching up various fruits and whipped cream to create a traditional English dessert. Use this quick hack and you will be mixing up wonderful flavor combinations to create delectable desserts for you and your friends.

I first had Eton Mess when I moved to England in 2006. I was at the Henley boat races in Oxford on a hotter-than-Hades summer day. A woman had brought a picnic basket with some treats in it and proceeded to mix up a big bowl of freshly whipped cream, fresh berries and crumbled meringue. I thought it was the best thing I'd ever tried, simple and refreshing!

Needless to say your imagination is all this dish is limited to.

You can do traditional: strawberries, raspberries and blueberries; or go wild with kiwi and mango! I usually add a small amount of vanilla extract or paste to the whipped cream but no sweetener since the meringue is so sweet, it makes for a nice balance of flavors.

CC'S SUNDAY BLUEBERRY PANCAKES

I LOVE Sunday brunch and I usually make a couple of dishes including one "speriment", as I call my kitchen trial basis cooking. This recipe made the cut when I tried it a couple of years ago. whipped egg whites add a lovely lightness and fluffiness to a lot of dishes, so I figured; why not pancakes? I have made these with strawberries, peaches and banana but my favorite is the blueberry version. Note: The banana was killer because I caramelized them in butter and brown sugar before adding to the pancake batter but that wasn't exactly "healthy". This recipe feeds up to 3 of your gaming crew.

0:05 PREP TIME

0:12 COOK TIME

3 SERVINGS

INGREDIENTS

3 large eggs, separated
1 cup full-fat Greek yogurt
3 Tbsp apple sauce or orange juice (trust me it works)
2½ Tbsp white or brown sugar (light or dark)
2 tsp vanilla extract
1 cup whole-wheat flour or ½ cup each of oat flour and white flour*
2½ tsp baking powder
¼ tsp salt
½ tsp cinnamon
1½ cups fresh blueberries
4 Tbsp butter, for the pan
Maple syrup, for serving

* or any flour combo that you like

METHOD

1. In a large bowl whisk together the egg yolks, Greek yogurt, applesauce or orange juice, brown sugar, and vanilla; set aside.

2. In a separate large bowl whisk together the flour, baking powder, salt, and cinnamon; and berries and toss to combine. Add flour mixture to the wet milky mixture and stir just to combine; do not over mix.

3. Add egg whites to a large bowl or the body of a stand mixer. Beat until you get soft but firm peaks. With a rubber spatula fold egg whites into the flour and wet ingredient mixture, stirring gently until egg whites are all nicely incorporated.

4. Melt two tablespoons of butter in a large skillet over medium heat. Ladle scoops of the batter into the skillet (whatever size you prefer your pancakes to be, I use about a quarter cup of batter per pancake) only cooking a few at a time so they don't stick together. Cook pancakes until the edges begin to brown and the top of the batter bubbles, then flip and cook for another 1-2 minutes. Repeat for all pancake batter. I like my pancakes with very crispy, buttery edges. Serve pancakes with maple syrup and extra berries and enjoy at once!

IN GAME DOWNLOADS

- YOU CAN MAKE OAT FLOUR SIMPLY BY PUTTING OATS INTO A FOOD PROCESSOR UNTIL FLOURLIKE CONSISTENCY.
- YOU CAN ALSO USE GLUTEN-FREE FLOUR OR RYE OR WHATEVER THE HECK YOU WANT.
- YOU CAN USE TWO PANS WITH 2 TABLESPOONS OF BUTTER IN EACH PAN, SO I CAN MAKE A LOT OF PANCAKES AT ONCE AND BE ABLE TO SIT DOWN AND ENJOY THEM WITH MY GUESTS!

"THE BANANA WAS KILLER BECAUSE I CARAMELIZED THEM IN BUTTER AND BROWN SUGAR BEFORE ADDING TO THE PANCAKE BATTER."

IN GAME DOWNLOADS

- TRY USING DIFFERENT FRUIT COMBINATIONS, BUT THE BANANA IS THE ONE MANDATORY INGREDIENT AS IT HELPS TO THICKEN SHAKE.
- DO NOT USE PINEAPPLE. IT WILL CURDLE THE MILK.
- FRUIT SUGGESTIONS ARE STRAWBERRIES, RASPBERRIES AND OTHER RIPE BERRIES.

PURPLE CLOUD BATTLE SHAKE

You're playing Blue Dragon and managing five friends in this turn-based RPG as they take on another evil overlord who rules over the Grand Kingdom, whose arrival is announced with purple clouds. All that fighting with your magical shadows — a dragon, a phoenix, a bat, a minotaur, or a saber-toothed tiger — is liable to make you thirsty. Try making this quick and tasty shake and Nene and his pals won't know what hit them!

Inspired by the video game Blue Dragon

0:05 PREP TIME

0:00 COOK TIME

2 SERVINGS

INGREDIENTS

Two cups blueberries
1 ripe banana
1–1½ cups milk

METHOD

1. Make sure blueberries are rinsed and de-stemmed then put into a blender.

2. Cut banana into rough pieces and put into blender along with milk.

3. Blend very well to make shake. Pour into cup and serve. Makes 2 servings.

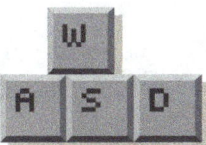

SNACKS

"Sometimes you just want a little nosh so make some of these tasty snacks ahead of time so you always have something on hand for hungry gamers!"

EXPLODUS POPCORNI

You've been running around in Lego Harry Potter, trying to not only defeat the One Who Shall Not Be Named, but also collect all the Lego bricks needed to open up new levels and characters. You have been playing quite a while, and you need something yummy to satisfy that late-afternoon hunger. Make some of this popcorn, and as quickly as you can say, "Explodus Popcorni", you can have homemade microwave popcorn! Now, instead of buying bags of microwave popcorn with loads of sodium and chemicals, why not save money and your health by making your own microwave popcorn? It's really easy, and fun to pick toppings too! Making popcorn stove top can be messy and dangerous with the hot oil splattering all over the place and not everyone has an air popper so this quick and easy hack makes fresh, hot popcorn available to just about anyone at any time! Just don't forget to wave that wand the right way when you use the incantation before making the popcorn!

0:01 PREP TIME

0:05 COOK TIME

2-4 SERVINGS

INGREDIENTS

¼ cup popcorn kernels

½ tsp oil

FLAVORS:

Parmesan cheese and garlic powder

Cinnamon and sugar

Chili mix or taco mix sprinkled on with melted butter

Your favorite hot sauce mixed with melted butter and poured over the popcorn

METHOD

1. Put the oil in the bottom of a large glass bowl or microwave safe bowl. Put a quarter cup of popcorn kernels in bowl on top of oil. Cover the bowl with plastic. Cut a couple of holes in the plastic wrap with a knife.

2. Put the bowl in the microwave, set it for 4-5 minutes (depending on your wattage) and wait for the kernels to pop.

3. When the pops slow down take out the popcorn. Please be careful the bowl will be very hot!

4. Put it in smaller bowls and make a few different flavors of popcorn.

Inspired by the video game Lego Harry Potter

"This quick and easy hack makes fresh, hot popcorn available to just about anyone at any time!"

IN GAME DOWNLOADS

- IF YOU WANT REALLY FINE SALT OR SUGAR FOR YOUR POPCORN, SEE THE HACK ON PAGE 183!

CLAUDIA & XAL'ATATH: BLADE OF THE BLACK EMPIRE

IN this incarnation of Warcraft I played Xal'atath, Blade of the Black Empire, an actual sword artifact for which the game is named. It's the weapon for World of Warcraft's Shadow Priest. I enjoy using my lower register to perform, my sexy voice. I used it in the beginning of Disney's Atlantis before Helga Sinclair turns into a badass soldier and I used it in the Gary Shandling Show when I did a take off of Kathleen Turner in Body Heat. In fact, I've been hired to do "sound alike" roles of Kathleen Turner, Angelina Jolie and Tilda Swindon. They all have terrific voices.

Maintaining that register through an entire production does put stress on your vocal cords but it's worth it when the final product sounds so good.

Blizzard invited me to BlizzCon in November of 2016. I got to do a panel with the actors and actresses from the game and the fans were just a hoot. Xal'atath proved to be a popular character and I had a fabulous time answering the questions in character.

"*I JUST REALIZED CLAUDIA CHRISTIAN IS THE VOICE OF MY WEAPON. I AM LITERALLY WIELDING SUSAN IVANOVA AGAINST MY FOES.*"

-MOVMENTARIAN, WORLD OF WARCRAFT COMMUNITY FORUM

XAL'ATATH'S MAD FRIES

Xal'atath is ancient, dating back to the Old Gods' Black Empire. Theories abound as to the nature of its creation, including claims that the blade is the remains of a forgotten Old God or even the claw of Y'shaarj itself. Whatever the truth of its origin, the blade is infused with the Old Gods' power. Legends state that it can even grant its wielder visions of the Black Empire, though doing so inevitably drives the viewer mad.

Ward off Xal'atath's maddening whispers with this ancient secret recipe – salty and sweet here's a treat you can't beat. Better make enough, because if there isn't enough for everyone, there may be a battle for the last fry and Xal'atath will whisper "Mmm, those fries are even more delicious, after you kill someone!"

Inspired by the video game World of Warcraft

- 0:05 PREP TIME
- 0:20 COOK TIME
- 4-8 SERVINGS

INGREDIENTS

- 2 large sweet potatoes
- 1–2 Tbsp olive oil (enough to coat fries), or oil of your choice
- 1 tsp garlic powder
- 1 tsp paprika (you can use regular or smoked paprika, you can also just use your favorite spice mix or herb blend)
- Salt and pepper, to taste

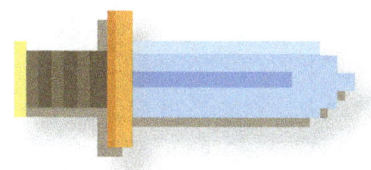

METHOD

1. Heat the oven to 425°. Cut the sweet potatoes into sticks ¼-inch wide and as long as French fries. Don't cut them too thin as they will burn, too thick they will be mushy. Mix the fries with the oil of your choice. You can use olive oil, coconut oil or whatever you like.

2. Then add the spices, salt and pepper and toss with the sweet potatoes. Spread them out on 2 rimmed baking sheets. I like to line the sheets with parchment to make clean up easier.

3. Make sure all of the fries are coated with the oil and spices, I use my hands to really rub it in (clean hands that is). Also ensure that there is space between each fry so they crisp up and not steam together into a wilted mass.

4. Bake until brown and crisp on the bottom, about 10 minutes, then flip and cook until the other side is crisp, about 10 minutes. Make sure you watch the fries in case they start to get too brown for your taste. Serve hot with the dipping sauce of your choice.

CONVENTION TRAIL MIX

You're making the eight-hour trek to a convention in another state. That Babylon 5 poster you have been attempting to get signed by the cast and creator is all but complete; there's just one more person to sign it, and you will finally have the crowning jewel to your Babylon 5 collection! While you are on the road, you will need something to nosh on, so you can keep up your energy on the long drive. Why not make some Convention Trail Mix to keep close at hand, so you can stave off those hunger pangs as you ponder getting that last signature.

0:05 PREP TIME

0:00 COOK TIME

6 SERVINGS

INGREDIENTS

1 cup peanuts
⅔ cup sunflower seeds
⅔ cup whole almonds
1 cup mini pretzels
1 cup wheat Chex Cereal (or any whole grain cereal)
⅔ cup M&M candies

METHOD

1. Place all ingredients into a large mixing bowl and mix gently with a spatula.

2. Once mixed, place trail mix into a re-sealable container and snack as desired. This recipe makes about 6 cups, enough for about 6 people.

IN GAME DOWNLOADS

- INSTEAD OF WHEAT CHEX CEREAL, TRY USING YOUR FAVORITE COLD BREAKFAST CEREAL OR EVEN SMALL SNACK CRACKERS. USE YOUR IMAGINATION AND TRY DIFFERENT NUTS OR SEEDS AS WELL!

TRIVIAL PIZZA MUFFINS

There's no need to use store bought pizza dough if you just have a couple of ingredients for this easy, fast, yummy pizza muffin recipe. Whether you're playing Minecraft or a rousing game of Trivial Pursuit Online, you can have this tasty treat made in no time at all, and you and your friends can gobble them up between or even during gaming sessions since they're perfect finger food! Makes 12 muffins – enough for up to 6 gamers to have 2 muffins each.

0:08 PREP TIME

0:20 COOK TIME

6-12 SERVINGS

IN GAME DOWNLOADS
- TRY ZUCCHINI RIBBONS FOR EXTRA HEALTHY MUFFINS (SEE PASTA HACKS P.151).

INGREDIENTS

1 cup flour
1 tsp baking soda
1 egg
1 cup milk
⅓ cup grated Parmesan
1 cup grated mozzarella (whole milk)
1 Tbsp Italian seasoning
¼ tsp red chili pepper flakes
½ cup extra toppings, such as pepperoni, cooked sausage or toasted vegetables (optional)

Inspired by Trivial Pursuit Online

METHOD

1. Stir all ingredients in a medium bowl until just blended.

2. Add half a cup of pepperoni or cooked sausage or chopped up toasted vegetables or just leave them as cheese flavored only.

3. Spray a mini muffin tin or regular size muffin tin with nonstick spray. Fill the muffin tins about ¾ of the way full then add some more pepperoni or sausage or chopped vegetables or whatever you're using to the top of the muffin dough.

4. Put in a 400° oven for about 20 minutes, enjoy!

HACK ATTACK!

PILLSBURY DOUGH HACK

If you don't have pizza dough or puff pastry, try this great substitute for a substantial snack!

Another great pizza hack is to use good quality focaccia bread as the "pizza crust" and cook it in a pan on the stove top. Simply put some oil in a non-stick pan, place a square of focaccia bread on the hot oil. Top with anything you want:

Cooked vegetables, fresh tomatoes, cheese, ham and pineapple, fresh herbs, sausage and marinara, cheeses... anything!

Cook for 5 minutes in the pan then transfer to a preheated oven with the broiler on to brown it up and melt any cheese you put on it, should take only a few minutes to brown so keep your eye on it.

Cut into wedges, sprinkle with cheese or season with salt and paper and fresh herbs or chili flakes and enjoy!

A GLAMOROUS MEAL AT THE RITZ HOTEL IN PARIS WITH MY GERMAN COUSIN, KATI.

205

RIOT CONTROL SEASONED PRETZELS

Looking for a different snack choice other than chips or candy? Why not make some of these seasoned pretzel pieces and share them with the other members of your T-Zero riot control crew? Something to munch on while beating back unruly members of the Burner gang. But be warned; if you don't make enough, you might find yourself thrown to the gangs!

0:06 PREP TIME

0:50 COOK TIME

4+ SERVINGS

INGREDIENTS

1 bag hard pretzels, unsalted
¾ cup oil
¼ tsp chipotle pepper powder
½ tsp salt
2 tsp garlic powder
2 tsp dill weed

METHOD

1. Preheat oven to 200°. Line a large baking sheet with parchment paper or a silicone baking mat.

2. Break the pretzels into pieces. Place pretzels in a large zipped-top bag. Add the oil and the spices. Shake it all together very well. Sometimes I shake it, let it sit for a minute, and shake it again. You want every piece coated very well. If you find there aren't enough spices coating the pretzels, add more spices to your taste.

3. Spread the pretzels onto the prepared baking sheet. If they don't all fit in a single layer, use two sheets. Bake for 50 minutes, making sure to stir the pretzels around a few times during baking. Remove from the oven and allow to cool.

The pretzels will stay fresh covered tightly at room temperature for 3 weeks, but odds are they won't last nearly that long!

Inspired by the video game Urban Chaos: Riot Response

IN GAME DOWNLOADS

- TRY USING LARGER-SIZED PRETZELS FOR BIGGER PIECES. YOU CAN ALSO TRY USING DIFFERENT SEASONING MIXES IN LIEU OF THE RANCH SEASONING OR LET YOUR IMAGINATION FLY AND MAKE YOUR OWN SEASONING MIX FOR BONUS ACHIEVEMENT POINTS!

OPEN SEASONED NUT RECIPE

Boog, Elliott and their friends are on an adventure to help Boog return to nature after having been among humans nearly all his life. They're trying to elude a mean hunter while teaching Boog how to be a wild bear. While there are lots of things to eat along the way, their friend McSquizzy, the squirrel, has introduced them to this tasty, nutty treat that will be gone almost as fast as open hunting season. Better grab a handful of these naughty but nice treats before they're all gone!

0:10 PREP TIME

0:20 COOK TIME

3 SERVINGS

INGREDIENTS

- ¼ cup brown sugar
- ¼-½ tsp cayenne pepper, depending on your heat level preference
- ½ tsp cinnamon
- ¼ tsp cumin (optional)
- 1 egg white
- 3 cups of your favorite assorted nuts (salted cashews, raw walnuts, dry roasted peanuts, pecan halves, hazelnuts, etc)
- ½ cup of your favorite dried fruit (cranberries or raisins for example)

METHOD

1. Preheat oven to 300°. In a small bowl, combine the brown sugar, cinnamon and cayenne and cumin, if using; set aside.

2. In a large bowl, whisk egg white; add nuts and cranberries. Sprinkle with sugar mixture and toss to coat.

3. Spread in a single layer on a greased baking sheet. If you have parchment paper, line the baking sheet with it, makes for an easier clean up. Bake for 18-20 minutes or until golden brown, stirring once. Cool. This recipe makes 3 servings of ¾ cup each. Store in an airtight container.

Inspired by the video game Open Season

IN GAME DOWNLOADS

- INSTEAD OF USING EGG WHITES TO COAT THE NUT MIX, SUBSTITUTE 2 TABLESPOONS OF GOOD OLIVE OIL, TOSS THE NUT MIXTURE AND BAKE AS IN STEP 3, BUT KEEP AN EYE ON THE NUTS SO THEY DON'T BURN!
- FOR A SAVORY VERSION (PICTURED), TRY THE FOLLOWING SPICE MIXTURE:
  - ¼ TEASPOON CHIPOTLE PEPPER POWDER
  - ½ TEASPOON PAPRIKA
  - 2 TABLESPOONS CHILI POWDER
  - 1 TEASPOON SALT
  - ½ TEASPOON PEPPER
  - 1 TEASPOON DRY MINCED ONIONS
  - ½ TEASPOON DRY THYME
- MIX NUTS WITH SPICES AND OLIVE OIL, THEN BAKE AS PER STEP 3, TOSS THE MIXTURE HALFWAY THROUGH THE COOKING TIME TO ENSURE NUTS COOK EVENLY, THEN SERVE.

HACK ATTACK!

CAN ATTACK

While you're making your sauces, try this can-opening hack to make opening those cans easier!

For as long as people have had cans, they've used can openers the same way: they latch onto the lid from its side and rotate the can opener around it. This nearly always leaves jagged edges both on the lid and the top of the can. But with the following hack, you can take the lid off, and leave a nice edge around the rim of the can and the lid (but just the same always be careful with metal edges).

First position the can opener parallel with the lid, not perpendicular. This may seem odd, but trust me, this will work. Latch onto the lid's rim and start cranking. It may take a few seconds more than the traditional way, but if you're patient, you will be rewarded by having a perfectly removed lid – rim and all! Simply rinse off the lid, place it into the recycle bin and then get on with your creating your magnificent snack.

LAVA BUCKET NUTS

In Minecraft lava can be a very useful item; you can smelt iron, cook up some raw meat, or create harder substances for building things – like an iron sword or golden armor. You can even use it to create obsidian blocks, which will allow you to travel into the mysterious (and dangerous) nether realm to face off against the dreaded nether dragon! Now you can make a tasty treat that is just as hot, but not as dangerous. Try making this nut recipe and you'll be able to satisfy your taste for something hot and savory. They're good by themselves, but just as useful on top of recipes! This recipe makes 2 servings but can be easily doubled to feed more of your Minecraft gaming friends.

0:01 PREP TIME

0:20 COOK TIME

2 SERVINGS

INGREDIENTS

1 cup unsalted cashews
4 Tbsp Sriracha sauce

METHOD

1. Heat oven to 300°. Combine cashews and Sriracha sauce in a small bowl and stir until nuts are coated.

2. Line a small baking pan with foil or parchment and spread the cashews out on it, then place in the oven and bake until nuts are dry, approximately 20 minutes.

3. Carefully remove the nuts and let cool. These nuts go really well with the curry chicken recipe (p.85) or just as a snack. If using in a recipe chop them up, if using as a snack, leave them whole.

Inspired by Minecraft because, you know, you can't be too inspired by Minecraft.

CRASHBREAKER CHIPS

One of my favorite games to play from time-to-time is the Burnout series of video games. You race around in an attempt to not only beat your opponents but cause them to crash, spectacularly! One of the most fun modes in the game is the crashbreaker mode. In this mode of the game you can cause massive multi-car pileups without really hurting anyone - but racking up a massive damage score while the in-game fans chant, "Crashbreaker, Crashbreaker, Crashbreaker". What would go great with an awesome game like Burnout? Some Crashbreaker chips! They're easy to make and taste much better than what you would get at the store. They pair really well with some Slime Dressing (p.160). Make some Crashbreaker Chips and see how high a score you can get.

Inspired by the video game Burnout Revenge

0:06 PREP TIME

0:18 COOK TIME

4 SERVINGS

INGREDIENTS

8 4-inch corn (or flour) tortillas
Cooking spray
Salt (to taste)

METHOD

1. Warm tortillas for 1 minute in microwave on a microwave-safe dish with 2 damp paper towels over tortillas.

2. Preheat oven to 400°. Spray larger plate with cooking spray and slide tortillas over the sprayed plate, coating both sides with spray.

3. Place tortilla on 2nd plate and season with salt (or your favorite seasoning mix). Repeat until all tortillas are greased and seasoned.

4. Use knife to cut through stack of tortillas to create 4 equal parts and place onto baking sheets.

5. Place in oven for 7 minutes, then flip and cook for another 7 to 10 minutes or until chips are crisp. Immediately transfer chips to bowl and enjoy!

IN GAME DOWNLOADS

- TRY USING DIFFERENT SEASONING MIXES TO FLAVOR YOUR CHIPS. THE ONES PHOTOGRAPHED WERE DUSTED WITH MESQUITE SEASONING, BUT ANY TYPE OF SEASONING WILL WORK WELL WITH THIS RECIPE. TRY MASHING UP DIFFERENT SEASONINGS TO CREATE YOUR OWN CRASHBREAKER SEASONING!

MAZE ROBOT HUMMUS

You're surrounded by alien robots who are chasing you as you attempt to make it out of their bizarre maze-like world. You have been running from the laser-blasting bots for what seems like forever, and you are feeling hungry. Why not make a batch of this out-of-this-world hummus to help keep you powered up for the long road ahead, or else you will go berserk!

0:10 PREP TIME

0:00 COOK TIME

2-3 SERVINGS

Inspired by the 1980 video game Berzerk on the Atari 2600

INGREDIENTS

2 cans chick peas
1 Tbsp minced garlic
⅔ cup olive oil
Pinch of salt
Fresh ground pepper (optional)
2 chipotle peppers in adobo sauce

METHOD

1. Rinse and drain chick peas. Put into food processor, along with garlic, olive oil, seasonings and adobo peppers.

2. Puree until the consistency you like. If mixture is too thick, add a teaspoon or two of water to thin, then serve. Goes well with pita chips, or Crashbreaker Chips (p.212), or even potato chips and pretzels!

IN GAME DOWNLOADS

- TRY USING VARIOUS SPICES TO FLAVOR THE HUMMUS DIFFERENTLY! SOME EXAMPLES WOULD BE TACO SEASONING, CHILI SEASONING, OR JUST GO BERSERK AND MAKE YOUR OWN SPICE BLEND TO ADD INTO THE HUMMUS!

IN GAME DOWNLOADS

- TRY COOKING THE EGGPLANT ON A GRILL INSTEAD OF ROASTING IN THE OVEN, FOR A "SMOKIER" FLAVOR.
- YOU CAN VARY THE AMOUNT OF GARLIC, OLIVE OIL, LEMON JUICE AND TAHINI TO TASTE.
- ALSO, YOU MAY ADD VARIOUS HERBS OR SPICES (SUCH AS GROUND HOT PEPPER, ETC.) TO KICK UP THE FLAVOR.

THE PRINCE'S HOMEMADE BABA GANOUSH

While the Sultan is away, his most-trusted advisor has seized power and locked his daughter, the Princess away in a tower. If she doesn't agree to be his wife, she will die, unless you — her true love — can escape your dungeon and come to her rescue. You face many obstacles along your path, and with all the running, jumping and dodging of various traps and enemies you will get hungry along the way. You can make this amazing dip, made with eggplant to help keep you on your toes. Serve it with some pita chips or pita crackers and you can munch while attempting to rescue the Princess!

0:02 PREP TIME

1:00 COOK TIME

2-4 SERVINGS

INGREDIENTS

1 large or 2 medium eggplants
Juice of 1 lemon
1 clove garlic, minced (or 1 Tbsp jarred minced garlic)
1–2 Tbsp olive oil
½ tsp sesame tahini
Salt and pepper, to taste

METHOD

1. Preheat oven to 400°. Do not peel the eggplant. Poke holes in the eggplant with a toothpick to allow steam to escape.

2. Cook eggplant on a sheet tray in oven at 400° for about an hour.

3. Let eggplant cool then peel away the skin. Use a spoon to remove the seed clusters (optional).

4. Chop eggplant and transfer to the bowl of a blender or food processor. Add remaining ingredients and process 10 seconds on low to blend all into a mixture, then 20 seconds on high to puree.

5. Adjust seasonings (optional: sprinkle with herbs of your choice). Chill. Serve with pita bread or chips.

Inspired by the video game The Prince of Persia

HACK ATTACK!

HARD-BOILED EGG HACKS

If you enjoy a good hard-boiled egg, there are two things that are a must; a hard-boiled egg that has no gray in it, and the ability to cleanly peel the shell off the egg. Here are a couple of hacks to make you an expert at hard-boiled eggs.

HACK #1: As I mentioned in My Secret Life as a Voice-Acting Food Hacker (p.5), there's a simple trick to making a nicely hard-boiled egg without any gray.

Put eggs in a pot, cover with cold water and bring to a boil (not too quickly, or they'll crack). Then, when the water is boiling, turn the heat off and stick a lid on the pot. After 10-13 minutes remove the lid and put the pot of eggs under cold running water until the water is cool.

HACK #2: Here's another hack to help you with peeling the shell off the egg. You can either peel the egg in a bath of water or, if you don't plan to use the boiled eggs right away, place them into a container (plastic container works well as long as it can be sealed) and start shaking the container vigorously. The shells will loosen away from the eggs and allow for a real easy peeling. Plus, most of the shells will be in the container and you can simply dump the shells into your compost pile or into the garbage!

RETRO GAMING: THE HOLY GRAIL OF INTELLIVISION ACCESSORIES

GAMERS love games. Whether it's playing on our favorite console, venturing out to games stores for the latest release, flea markets to track down retro items for our collection or even conventions and esports events, we can't get enough!

One of the crowning jewels in my collection—A Mattel Intellivision music keyboard!

It was 2008 and I was in the midst of building my video game collection up for the third time. I'd never been to a game convention before so my buddy John threw my manual wheelchair (I used the chair for outings like that the time) into his car and we made the 40-minute trek from my apartment to the annual Too Many Games convention in King of Prussia, Pennsylvania. It's like most cons; there are dealers who have various consoles and assorted titles available for purchase. There are also gaming guests, which may be a voice talent, programmer, or even an internet sensation whose net series deals with old video games. We arrived on the last day of the show. John found a sweet wood grain veneer 4-switch Atari 2600, complete with the smoke-colored system organizer.

I happened on a table that had a bunch of loose cartridges for the Atari and Nintendo. The dealer also had something I never thought I would see in the wild—a Mattel Intellivision music keyboard! This bad boy was a thing of beauty. Three feet long, a full-size synthesizer keyboard. My gamer heart skipped a beat as I made my way over to it. The dealer, who had been at the show all weekend, looked like he was ready to pack up and head home. I knew this awesome piece of gaming history was priced at around $80 - $90, if you could even find it. He looked at me in the wheelchair as I checked out the keyboard. "Do you have a way to get the keyboard home with you?" he asked.

> "*I* KNEW THIS AWESOME PIECE OF GAMING HISTORY WAS PRICED AT AROUND $80 - $90, IF YOU COULD EVEN FIND IT."

"I can probably find a way if the price is right," I replied.

"How does fifty dollars sound?"

I gave him a wrinkled look of uncertainty.

"I really don't want to lug this thing back home with me," he confided, "so I'll tell you what I'll do. If you can get this home, I'll let you have it for $25."

I couldn't put the money in his hand fast enough. My friend John saw me wheeling around with my prize. When I told him what the Intellivision keyboard was and what I'd paid for it, and he was floored! To this day, it's is one of my most prized gaming possessions.

GAME CONVENTION DEVILED EGGS

You and your gaming buddies have finally gotten tickets for PAX East and have been in line for the convention for quite a while. You still have a while to wait until the doors open, and you and your buddies are starting to get hungry. Good thing you made some of these wonderful deviled eggs to bring on your trek! They'll be all gone by the time you finally reach the entrance to the convention!

0:05 PREP TIME

0:15 COOK TIME

6 SERVINGS

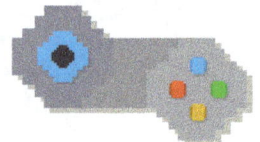

INGREDIENTS

- 12 eggs (any size)
- ½ cup mayonnaise
- 2 tsp mustard (Dijon, yellow or grainy)
- 1 tsp pickles, chopped
- 1 tsp capers, chopped
- ¼ tsp chives, chopped
- ¼ tsp dill, chopped
- Pinch of paprika, for garnish
- Pinch of salt
- 4 slices cooked bacon chopped, for garnish

METHOD

1. Hard-boil the eggs (13 minutes using hack on page 218) then run under cold water and allow to cool completely.

2. While eggs are cooling, take bacon and cook until crisp. Remove from pan and place on paper towels to remove excess grease and set aside.

3. Peel eggs then slice them along the side and remove yolks and place yolks into a mixer. Put the empty halves of eggs off to the side.

4. Put all other ingredients into the blender and mix well until mixture is creamy and smooth. Take mixture out of blender and place into a plastic resealable bag and seal tightly. Snip off the end of the bag to form a piping tip and pipe the filling into the white parts of the egg. There should be enough mixture to fill all of the shells evenly.

5. Slice down bacon and place 1 or 2 slices into the top of each egg half. Sprinkle paprika on tops for curb appeal and serve.

IN GAME DOWNLOADS

- FOR AN UPSCALE LOOK AND TASTE, TRY TOPPING THE DEVILED EGGS WITH SALMON ROE OR EVEN CAVIAR!
- CAN ALSO TOP WITH GREEN ONIONS, OR THINLY SLICED LOX OR PROSCIUTTO.

IN GAME DOWNLOADS

- YOU CAN SUBSTITUTE ANY DELI MEAT IN LIEU OF PEPPERONI.
- CAN ALSO SUBSTITUTE PROVOLONE CHEESE FOR THE SHREDDED MOZZARELLA.
- FOR A SPICIER PIZZA, TRY ADDING 1 SLICE OF EITHER JALAPEÑO PEPPER OR BANANA HOT PEPPER OR YOUR FAVORITE SPICES INTO DOUGH BEFORE BAKING.
- SERVE WITH A SIDE OF WARMED MARINARA AND NOT MISS A BEAT WHEN GOING UP AGAINST THE COVENANT.

HEALTH PACK PIZZA PICK-UPS

When you're fighting off Covenant in Halo, you'll need your strength quickly without too much prep work, and you want to be able to have a hand free to target your enemies while tossing back one of these pizza rolls into your mouth. These mini pizza rolls are easy to eat on the fly and give you an added gaming boost that even Cortana would approve. This recipe makes enough for up to 3 gamers to enjoy while fighting off the Covenant hordes!

Inspired by the video game Halo

0:05 PREP TIME

0:19 COOK TIME

3 SERVINGS

INGREDIENTS

1 tube pizza dough
6 oz pepperoni slices
8 oz shredded mozzarella cheese
Marinara sauce (optional)

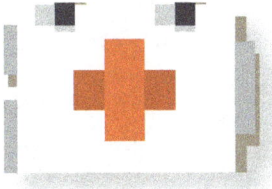

METHOD

1. Pre-heat oven to 400°. Spray a 9x13 baking sheet with non-stick spray. Unroll pizza dough onto sheet. Cut dough with dough cutter into circles.

2. On each circle, place a teaspoon of marinara sauce in the middle (if using) then 1 slice of pepperoni and top with shredded mozzarella.

3. Fold circle over to form a half-moon and crimp to seal. Repeat process until all dough disks are formed into half-moons.

4. Bake for 19 minutes until golden.

DEEP SEA KAIJU QUICK TUNA MELT

After a long day of city wrecking and destroying everything before you with your atomic heat beam it's time to take a refreshing dip in the ocean. Hang on, there are sea kaiju? Here comes Ebirah, Horror of the Deep! No sweat, you can breathe underwater, pummel him into submission and then finish him off topside with your atomic heat breath to make a kaiju tuna melt. You're going to need a lot of soup crackers to use up all that deep sea kaiju tuna.

Inspired by the video game Godzilla: Unleashed

0:02 PREP TIME

0:01 COOK TIME

1-2 SERVINGS

INGREDIENTS

6–7 round soup crackers

2½ oz of your favorite ready-made or homemade tuna salad or 1 deep sea kaiju (optional)

1 package (4 oz) grated cheese (mozzarella in this case)

METHOD

1. Place crackers on a microwave-safe dish, spoon just enough tuna mixture to just cover cracker, then put some grated cheese on top.

3. Repeat until all crackers are covered and place into microwave for 30 seconds.

4. Remove and serve immediately.

AELA'S GRILLED CHEESE

You have been wandering around the world of Skyrim for what seems like weeks, trying to locate that one magical item you need to finish a recent quest when suddenly, you are besieged by a rolling mass of goat cheese wheels heading down a mountain straight for you! You could run in a vain attempt to save yourself, or you could gather as many cheese wheels as you can so you can make these tasty grilled cheese sandwiches and finish out your quest on a full stomach!

PS: Keep an eye out for the following charcters voiced by Claudia: Aela the Huntress, Legate Rikke, Adelaisa Vendicci, Adrianne Avenicci, Breya, Brina Merilis, Bryling, Faleen, Iona, Laila Law-Giver, Potema Septim, Rayya, Sorli the Builder, Uthgerd the Unbroken, Voldsea Giryon, and Zaria.

Inspired by the video game Elder Scrolls V: Skyrim

0:05 PREP TIME

0:10 COOK TIME

1 SERVINGS

INGREDIENTS

2–4 slices of bread

½ tsp butter at room temperature (you can substitute mayonnaise, favorite aioli, or mustard instead of butter)

3–4 slices deli meat (I used corned beef)

2 slices of your favorite cheese (I used 1 slice of cheddar and 1 slice of mozzarella for this recipe)

¼ tsp jalapeño peppers, diced (optional)

Cooking spray

METHOD

1. Spray pan with light amount of cooking spray and heat to low setting. Spread butter onto one side of bread, then place into heated pan with the butter side down.

2. Place 1 slice of cheese on top of bread, then the meat, jalapeño peppers, if using, and 2nd piece of cheese.

3. Butter the other piece of bread on one side, and place with butter side up.

4. When lower piece of cheese begins to melt, flip the whole sandwich carefully over to other side and cook until cheese is melty and gooey. Remove from pan and enjoy!

226

IN GAME DOWNLOADS

- TRY USING DIFFERENT TYPES OF CHEESE, LIKE PEPPER JACK, MONTEREY JACK, PROVOLONE OR EVEN GOAT CHEESE FOR A DIFFERENT CHEESE FLAVOR.
- ALSO TRY USING DIFFERENT CUTS OF DELI MEAT OR EVEN DICED CHICKEN OR TUNA.

CLAUDIA CHRISTIAN has had a lifelong passion for cooking. She has also starred as a voice actor in games like Call of Duty, World of Warcraft, Starcraft, Guild Wars, Fallout 4, Halo and Skyrim and as Helga Sinclair in Disney's Atlantis. Claudia landed her first studio film at 20 in the cult hit The Hidden. Christian went on to star in over fifty films such as Clean and Sober with Morgan Freeman and Michael Keaton, and hundreds of TV shows including the sci-fi megahit Babylon 5. She is the author of her addiction memoir Babylon Confidential and the co-author of the science fiction novel Wolf's Empire.

Claudia Christian stands out as a public figure that uses her platform to not only share her many talents but also to stand up as a spokesperson for alternative treatments for alcoholism. As head of the C3 Foundation and author of books like her addiction memoir Babylon Confidential, Claudia has promoted The Sinclair Method and helped saved countless lives. Her TedX talk How I Overcame Alcoholism has over 2,000,000 views.

For more information visit

cthreefoundation.org or
claudiachristian.net

MARK MICHEL is a writer, gamer and photographer. specializing in nature and flower photography. Mark details how his gaming experience, cooking ability and ingenious life hacks help him deal with the limitations of his cerebral palsy. He provided much of the food photography in Snack Hacks and can be found on Xbox Live where he enjoys Halo, Minecraft and Crackdown 3 among others.

INDEX OF RECIPES

APPETIZERS 9

Ambigram Palmiers — 22
Bricky Nachos — **14**,15
Dragon Kickers Chicken — 20,**21**
Ham & Cheese Puffball Pie — 16
Stealthy Mouse Cheese Puffs — 24
Totally Loco Mini Taco Bowls — 10,**11**
Warhog Bacon-Wrapped Pineapple Bites — 13

SOUPS & SALADS 27

Chicken Chaser Chicken Salad Roll — 48,**49**
CC's Southwest Grilled Corn & Black Bean Buckshot Salad — 52
Farm Fresh Watermelon Cucumber Salad — 41
Garden War Tomato-Basil Soup — **28**,29
Ivanova's Russian Borsht — 46
King of Red Lions Veggie Soup — 34,**35**
Pellet 3-Bean Salad — 40
Plumber Power Gazpacho — **38**,39
Stunt Driver's Corn Chowder Soup — 32,**33**
TRace-On Code Slaw — 50,**51**

MAINS 55

Anti-Dracula Garlic Chicken — 82,**83**
Arthur's Spicy Asian Meat Buns with Bok Choy Slaw — 123
Best of Show Watch Party Chili — 56,**57**
Billy Egg's Spicy–Tangy Chicken Thighs — 78
Breakaway Hockey Chicken Parmesan — **76**,77
Captain Ferran's On-the-Go Chicken Wraps — 111
Catch of the Day Tuna Burgers — 113
CC's Crazy Goat Lamb Shanks with Polenta — 66
Dragon Born Burnt Hand Chicken — 89
Dragon Power Mac & Cheese — 122
Freeway Chicken Madras — **84**,85
Hail to the King Hamburgers — 108,**109**
Helga's Ceviche — 98,**99**
High Octane Breakfast Hub Caps — **104**,105
Hop Along Enchiladas — 114,**115**
Quick Metro Chicken Kiev — **70**,71
Rapture Deep Sea Salmon — 79
Recording Booth Sausage & Peppers — 106,**107**
Skills for Kills Grilled Skirt Steak — 58
Slingshot Pork Brine — 68
Space Shooter Roasted Chicken — 74
Sport Fish Halibut with Cabbage & Potatoes — 92
Surviving Cryostasis Spaghetti — 60,**61**
The Furious Five's Salmon Foil Meal — 94,**95**
The Game Winner! — 102
The Philly Special Cheesesteak — **116**,117
VFX Power Sloppy Joes — 120,**121**
Westballz Meatballz — **64**,65

VEGGIES & SIDES 125

Amaizing Roasted Corn — 147
Beta-Tester Baked Potatoes — 137
Born to Grill Twice-Baked Potatoes — **132**,133
Easy Harvest Cauliflower Steaks — 138,**139**
Ghost Busting Eggplant Parmesan — 126,**127**
Quick Pepper Side — 146
Rash and Bash Super Onion — 142,**143**
Roasted Pursuit Whole Cauliflower — 140
Sporty California Easy Zucchini Pasta — 130,**131**

DRESSINGS & SAUCES 149

Addictively Sweet Jalapeño Rocket Relish — 156,**157**
CC's "Just for the Halibut" Sauce — 155
War God Salad Dressing — 159
Epic Perky Pesto — 150
Farmer's Bounty Hot Pepper Relish — 158
Slime Dressing — 160,**161**
Sunday Afternoon Smash Tomato Gravy — 152,**153**

DESSERTS & SWEETS   163

Anti-Dalek Keto Brownies	184
Badass Cookies!	186,**187**
Banana Hoard Ice Cream	173
Purple Cloud Battle Shake	**194**,195
Bullet Combo Chocolate Brownies	180,**181**
CC's Sunday Blueberry Pancakes	192,**193**
Claudia's Fairy Godmother Cookies	188,**189**
Claudia's Deadly Disc Summer Citrus Pie	177
Dancing Penguin Easy Vanilla Ice Cream	171
Hot Top Molten Chocolate Cake	178,**179**
Mad Bomber Apple Pie Poppers	164,**165**
Pacnana Ice Cream Pie	174,**175**
Turner and Landau Caramel Sauce	168

SNACKS   197

Aela's Grilled Cheese	226,**227**
Convention Trail Mix	202,**203**
Crashbreaker Chips	212,**213**
Deep Sea Kaiju Quick Tuna Melt	224,**225**
Explodus Popcorn!	198,**199**
Game Convention Deviled Eggs	220,**221**
Health Pack Pizza Pick-Ups	**222**,223
Lava Bucket Nuts	211
Maze Robot Hummus	214,**215**
Open Seasoned Nut Recipe	208,**209**
Riot Control Seasoned Pretzels	206,**207**
The Prince's Homemade Baba Ganoush	**216**,217
Trivial Pizza Muffins	204
Xal'atath's Mad Fries	**200**,201

HACK ATTACKS

Hack attack: Baconator	23
Hack attack: Butter Portions	**136**
Hack attack: Can Attack	**210**
Hack attack: Claudia's Daily Hacks	30
Hack attack: Faking Fancy Puff Pastry 1.0	23
Hack attack: Faking Fancy Puff Pastry 2.0	176
Hack attack: Fancy 5-minute Scallops	**100,101**
Hack attack: Hacks for Pasta	151
Hack attack: Hacky Parchment Paper	59
Hack attack: Hard-Boiled Egg Hacks	218
Hack attack: Hello Halo!	128
Hack attack: Herbs and Fancy French Herbs	90
Hack attack: Muffin Tin Taco Hack	**12**
Hack attack: No Machine Ice Cream	172
Hack attack: One Pan Meals	118
Hack attack: Perfectly Cooked Fish Hack	154
Hack attack: Pickled Onions	37
Hack attack: Pillsbury Dough Hack	205
Hack attack: Powdered Sugar	183
Hack attack: Quick Buttermilk	69
Hack attack: Spinach Attack	144,**145**
Hack attack: Dessert Hack: Eton Mess	**190**,191
Hack attack: Waste Not Roasted Chicken	75
Hack attack: Wrap Hacks	112

NOTE: Numbers in bold indicate recipe pages with accompanying photos.

UNITS: We use degrees (°) Farenheit for the oven temperatures, pints (pt), pounds (lb), and ounces (oz), and American cups, tablespoons (Tbsp) and teaspoons (tsp).

GRAPHICS & PHOTO CREDITS

8 Bit Pixel Art Icons by Freepik.com

Hud Elements graphics by Vecteezy.com

Cover Photo & p. 196 by Nick Mendoza www.nickmendoza.biz

Photos pp. 4,8,26,51,54,84,91,115,118,124,148,153,162,170,181,182,190 and 199 by Chris Loomis www.chrisloomis.com

Photos pp. 7,11,12,14,21,33,35,38,70,76,81,95,104,107,109,116,121,127,132,139,143,157,161,165,175,189,194,203,207,209,213, 215,216,219,221,222,225 and 227 by Mark Michel

Photo of Weston Dennis, p.62 by Exilexi*

Photos of Gary Hudson p.72-73 courtesy of Gary Hudson

Photo of Robin Atkin Downes, p.86 courtesy of Robin Atkin Downes

Photo of Robin Atkin Downes, p.88 by Gage Skidmore**

Photo of Cas Anvar, p. 134 courtesy of Cas Anvar

Photo of Cas Anvar, p.135 by Gage Skidmore (photo cropped)***

Photo of Kathleen Turner, p. 166 by Kingkongphoto & www.celebrity-photos.com***

Other photos courtesy of Claudia Christian & Mark Michel

*This file is licensed under the Creative Commons Attribution- ShareAlike 4.0 International License.

** This file is licensed under the Creative Commons Attribution-Share Alike 3.0 Unported license.

***This file is licensed under the Creative Commons Attribution-Share Alike 2.0 Generic license.

FLOATING WORLD PRESS

Floating World press is dedicated to publishing unusual, interesting and enlightening books that help readers look at life and the world in a new, unexpected way.

Floating World Press, books for a better world.

For more information visit www.floatingworldpress.com

FLOATING WORLD PRESS

CPSIA information can be obtained
at www.ICGtesting.com
Printed in the USA
LVHW061332110619
620854LV00006B/163/P

9 780648 283195